A Confederate Lady Comes of Age

Pauline DeCaradeuc (courtesy of the Georgia Historical Society).

A Confederate Lady
Comes of Age

The Journal of Pauline DeCaradeuc Heyward,
1863-1888

edited by Mary D. Robertson

University of South Carolina Press

Women's Diaries and Letters of the Nineteenth-Century South

Carol Bleser, Series Editor

A WOMAN DOCTOR'S CIVIL WAR:
Esther Hill Hawks' Diary
edited by Gerald Schwartz

A REBEL CAME HOME:
The Diary and Letters of Floride Clemson, 1863–1866
edited by Ernest McPherson Lander, Jr., and Charles M. McGee, Jr.

THE SHATTERED DREAM:
The Day Book of Margaret Sloan, 1900–1902
edited by Harold Woodell

GEORGE WASHINGTON'S BEAUTIFUL NELLY:
The Letters of Eleanor Parke Custis Lewis to Elizabeth Bordley Gibson, 1794–1851
edited by Patricia Brady

A CONFEDERATE LADY COMES OF AGE:
The Journal of Pauline DeCaradeuc Heyward, 1863–1888
edited by Mary D. Robertson

Copyright © 1991 University of South Carolina

Published in Columbia, South Carolina, by the
University of South Carolina Press

Published 1991
First Paperback Edition 1997

Manufactured in the United States of America

01 00 99 98 97 6 5 4 3 2

ISBN 1–57003–228–9
Library of Congress Catalog Card Number 91–25091

For Mason,
who is always there for me

Contents

The Journal of Pauline DeCaradeuc Heyward
1863

1864

Illustrations

Pauline DeCaradeuc   *Frontispiece*

Following page 71

Montmorenci, the DeCaradeuc Home
Near Aiken, South Carolina

Pauline's Grandfather,
Jean Baptiste Ursule Laurent DeCaradeuc

Pauline's Parents, James Achille DeCaradeuc
and Elizabeth Ann della Torre DeCaradeuc

Jacob Guerard Heyward, circa 1861

Guerard's parents, George Cuthbert Heyward and
Elizabeth Martha Guerard Heyward

James Achille DeCaradeuc

Pauline DeCaradeuc Heyward
and Jacob Guerard Heyward, circa 1885

The Heyward Family, 1897

Series Editor's Introduction

A Confederate Lady Comes of Age: The Journal of Pauline DeCaradeuc Heyward, 1863–1888 is the fifth volume in an ongoing series of women's diaries and letters of the nineteenth-century South. In this series published by the University of South Carolina Press will be a number of never-before-published diaries, some collections of unpublished correspondence, and a few reprints of published diaries—a potpourri of nineteenth-century women's writings.

The Women's Diaries and Letters of the Nineteenth-Century South Series enables women to speak for themselves providing readers with a rarely opened window into Southern society before, during, and after the American Civil War. The significance of these letters and journals lies not only in the personal revelations and the writing talents of these women authors but also in the range and versatility of their contents. Taken together these publications will tell us much about the heyday and the fall of the Cotton Kingdom, the mature years of the "peculiar institution," the war years, and the adjustment of the South to a new social order following the defeat of the Confederacy. Through these writings the reader will also be presented with firsthand accounts of everyday life and social events, courtships and marriages, family life and travels, religion and education, and the life-and-death-matters which made up the ordinary and extraordinary world of the nineteenth-century South.

A Confederate Lady Comes of Age begins at Montmorenci near Aiken, South Carolina, where nineteen-year-old Pauline DeCaradeuc began keeping a journal in June 1863, just one month before the Confederate defeats at both Gettysburg and Vicksburg. Pauline's journal chronicles not only events on the battlefield but also the struggles of Southern families as they sought to carry on their daily lives in the face of the conflict.

Pauline had come of age during the hardship and tragedy of the Civil War. Her book records the loss of her youthful suitors in battle, and how, in the summer of 1865, soon after the war had ended, Pauline met the socially prominent South Carolinian Guerard Heyward who had spent the last two years as a prisoner of war.

Although the war had taken a heavy personal and economic toll of both the DeCaradeuc and Heyward families, the marriage of Pauline to Guerard took place in November 1866 amidst high expectations of future happiness and affluence.

Pauline's postwar journal records the couple's attempt to achieve a comfortable lifestyle in the post-Reconstruction era, their enduring love for one another, and the role of Pauline as a devoted mother of nine children in late-nineteenth-century Southern society.

Carol Bleser

Preface

South Carolinian Pauline DeCaradeuc (1843–1914) made her first journal entry on June 2, 1863, just one month before the fall of Vicksburg, Mississippi, following a siege of more than six weeks. The war had already brought great sorrow to the DeCaradeuc family. Pauline's brothers, Frank and Tonio, victims of typhoid fever, a common camp disease, had died in November and December of the preceding year.

Following the example set by her father, Achille, nineteen-year-old Pauline began recording the events of her times. Her journal spans the years 1863–1867 and 1875–1888, and thus serves as an important historical chronicle. But of even greater significance, perhaps, is the fact that her journal reveals the very private and intimate thoughts and feelings of an intelligent, cultured Southern woman about the society of her day and her role as a woman in that society.

My efforts to locate the original journal manuscript were unsuccessful. Fortunately, the Georgia Historical Society had a copy of Pauline's journal transcribed by her daughter, Maude Heyward, a former librarian at the Georgia Historical Society/ Chatham County Public Library in Savannah. Desiring that other family members should know her mother, Maude Heyward had thirty copies of her unannotated transcription privately printed and distributed in 1928. It is upon this transcription that I have based my work.

I am grateful for the transcriptionist's sense of history, which, presumably, resulted in a reproduction of the journal with few, if any, emendations. This editor has likewise intruded as little as possible into the body of the text in order to retain the authenticity and historical flavor of the original manuscript. Pauline's spelling, capitalizations, and punctuation in almost every instance have been followed. Her underlined words and phrases have been italicized, and all of her exclamatory punctuation retained. Only minor changes in spelling, punctuation, and dates have been made when deemed necessary for the sake of clarity or to correct the few obvious errors in transcription. Footnotes have been provided for purposes of explication and to present the journal in its historical setting.

To make the journal more readable I have divided the text into chapters, and selected chapter titles in keeping with the mood of the author and the recorded events of her times.

It would be impossible to mention here the many individuals who have contributed to the completion of this book. My research efforts were greatly facilitated by the staffs of the following institutions: the Southern Historical Collection, Wilson Library at the University of North Carolina; the South Carolina Historical Society, especially Cam Alexander and Kathleen Howard; the Charleston Library Society, especially Patricia G. Bennett; Bryan McKown, Paul Begley, and Patrick McCawley at the South Carolina Department of Archives and History; the South Caroliniana Library, especially Thelma Hayes; the Manuscript Division of Alderman Library at the University of Virginia; Tracy Bearden, Eileen Ielmini, and Jan Flores at the Georgia Historical Society; the Lane Library at Armstrong State College; the Aiken County Public Library, especially Sally Farris, reference librarian; Diane W. Timmerman and Katherine Scavens at the Edgefield, South Carolina, Courtesy Center and Archives; the Fannie Bayly King Staunton Public Library; Sue Rainey, reference librarian, the Hilton Head Branch Library of Beaufort County; the Beaufort County Public Library, especially Hillary Barnwell; Kathleen Robertson, reference librarian at the Savannah–Chatham County Public Library; Jerry Simmons, archivist at the Catholic Archives, Savannah; and the Chatham County Department of Vital Records, especially Linda Waters and Mary Logan.

I am also greatly appreciative of the help of a number of DeCaradeuc and Heyward family members. I wish to thank particularly John Smallbrook Howkins III of Biloxi, Mississippi, for his interest and generous help. I am grateful for his assistance in clarifying his branch of the family tree and for providing me with copies of numerous DeCaradeuc–Heyward family pictures and papers. Alice Heyward graciously received me and my photographer husband into her lovely old home in Bluffton, South Carolina, to make copies of portraits of George Cuthbert Heyward and his wife, Elizabeth Martha Guerard Heyward. In addition, she entrusted to me for purposes of research her copy of *The Heyward Family*. I am greatly appreciative of all her kindnesses. I also wish to thank D. Hasell Heyward, Jr., of Bluffton, Marjory Heyward Mingledorff of Savannah, and John H. Howkins of Atlanta for sharing with me their knowledge of the DeCaradeuc–Heyward family. Mary DeCaradeuc Bartholomew provided most gracious help in clarifying the della Torre/DeCaradeuc genealogy and in sharing her family pictures, documents, and history.

I am also indebted to Charlotte J. Shelton, friend and fellow historian, for her advice and counsel.

To my dear family, Mason, Mary Lynn, Bill, and Susan, I wish to express my gratitude for their encouragement and support over the years of all my endeavors. My special thanks go to my daughter Susan Kuzia, a marvelous research assistant, who journeyed to Aiken, Charleston, and Columbia with me for some intense archival research, and without whom I would never have completed this work. I also wish to thank my husband, Mason, for his enduring patience, especially as my mentor in understanding the arcane mysteries of the word processor, and for serving as my official photographer and general factotum. To my daughter Mary Lynn Zirkle go my thanks for always being there to lend a sympathetic ear. I wish to express my eternal gratitude to my son, Bill Robertson, and his spouse, Claire Pomeroy, for setting me up in a great workplace, which has greatly simplified my life and enabled me to complete this book.

Lastly, I wish to express my appreciation to Carol Bleser, Kathryn and Calhoun Lemon Distinguished Professor of History, Clemson University, for her friendship over the years, for persuading me to undertake this project, and for her help in finalizing this work.

Abbreviations

CMH   *Confederate Military History,* Clement Evans, ed. (Atlanta: 1899; New York: 1862)

GHS   Georgia Historical Society, Hodgson Hall, Savannah

OR   *War of the Rebellion: A Compilation of the Official Records of the Union and Confederate Armies* (Washington: Government Printing Office, 1880–1901)

ORN   *War of the Rebellion: The Official Records of the Union and Confederate Navies* (Washington: Government Printing Office, 1897)

SCHS   South Carolina Historical Society, Fireproof Building, Charleston

SCL   South Caroliniana Library, University of South Carolina, Columbia

SHC   Southern Historical Collection, Wilson Library, University of North Carolina, Chapel Hill

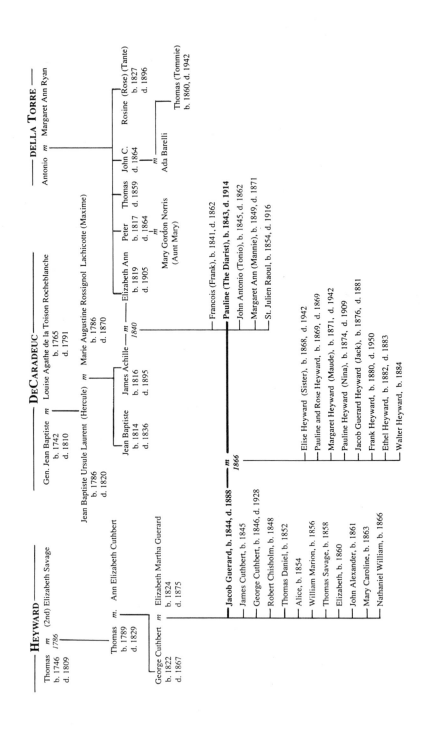

HEYWARD

Thomas *m* (2nd) Elizabeth Savage
b. 1746   *1786*
d. 1809

Thomas *m.* Ann Elizabeth Cuthbert
b. 1789
d. 1829

George Cuthbert *m* Elizabeth Martha Guerard
b. 1822   b. 1824
d. 1867   d. 1875

Jacob Guerard, b. 1844, d. 1888 ——— *m*
  │   *1866*
  ├─ James Cuthbert, b. 1845
  ├─ George Cuthbert, b. 1846, d. 1928
  ├─ Robert Chisholm, b. 1848
  ├─ Thomas Daniel, b. 1852
  ├─ Alice, b. 1854
  ├─ William Marion, b. 1856
  ├─ Thomas Savage, b. 1858
  ├─ Elizabeth, b. 1860
  ├─ John Alexander, b. 1861
  ├─ Mary Caroline, b. 1863
  └─ Nathaniel William, b. 1866

DeCaradeuc

Gen. Jean Baptiste   *m*   Louise Agathe de la Toison Rocheblanche
b. 1742   b. 1765
d. 1810   d. 1791

Jean Baptiste Ursule Laurent (Hercule)   *m*   Marie Augustine Rossignol Lachicotte (Maxime)
b. 1786   b. 1786
d. 1820   d. 1870

Jean Baptiste   James Achille ——— *m* ———   Elizabeth Ann   Peter   Thomas   John C.
b. 1814   b. 1816   *1840*   b. 1819   b. 1817   d. 1859   d. 1864
d. 1836   d. 1895   d. 1905   d. 1864
                                                                       m
                                                   Mary Gordon Norris
                                                      (Aunt Mary)

  ├─ Francois (Frank), b. 1841, d. 1862
  ├─ **Pauline (The Diarist), b. 1843, d. 1914**
  ├─ John Antonio (Tonio), b. 1845, d. 1862
  ├─ Margaret Ann (Mannie), b. 1849, d. 1871
  └─ St. Julien Raoul, b. 1854, d. 1916

  ├─ Elise Heyward (Sister), b. 1868, d. 1942
  ├─ Pauline and Rose Heyward, b. 1869, d. 1869
  ├─ Margaret Heyward (Maude), b. 1871, d. 1942
  ├─ Pauline Heyward (Nina), b. 1874, d. 1909
  ├─ Jacob Guerard Heyward (Jack), b. 1876, d. 1881
  ├─ Frank Heyward, b. 1880, d. 1950
  ├─ Ethel Heyward, b. 1882, d. 1883
  └─ Walter Heyward, b. 1884

DELLA TORRE

Antonio   *m*   Margaret Ann Ryan

Rosine (Rose) (Tante)
b. 1827
d. 1896

Ada Barelli
  m

Thomas (Tommie)
b. 1860, d. 1942

Principal Characters
Mentioned in the Journal

DeCaradeuc Family Members

James Achille DeCaradeuc (Fa), owner of Montmorenci,
Pauline DeCaradeuc Heyward's father

Elizabeth Ann della Torre DeCaradeuc (Mother), wife of Achille
DeCaradeuc; Pauline DeCaradeuc Heyward's mother

Francois (Frank) DeCaradeuc (Brother), Pauline's older brother;
died in the Confederate service in 1862

John Antonio DeCaradeuc (Tonio), Pauline's younger brother,
died in the Confederate service in 1862

Margaret Ann DeCaradeuc (Mannie), Pauline's younger sister

St. Julien Raoul DeCaradeuc, Pauline's brother,
the youngest of the family

Marie Augustine Rossignol (Maxime) Lachicotte DeCaradeuc
(Grandmother), Pauline's paternal grandmother, widow of
Jean Baptiste Ursule (Hercule) Laurent DeCaradeuc, living
at Montmorenci with the family

The della Torre Family

Margaret Ann Ryan della Torre (Ma), Pauline's maternal
grandmother, widow of Antonio della Torre

Rose della Torre (Tante), Pauline's beloved aunt living
at Montmorenci

John C. della Torre (Uncle John), Pauline's uncle, married to Ada Barelli, father of Thomas della Torre

Thomas della Torre (Tommie), Pauline's little nephew, living with the DeCaradeucs at Montmorenci

Peter della Torre (Uncle Peter), Pauline's uncle, married to Mary Gordon Norris of Maryland

Eliza Ryan McDonald (Daughter), Pauline's maternal great-aunt, married to Dr. J. C. W. McDonald and living at nearby Rose Hill

The Heyward Family

George Cuthbert and Elizabeth Martha Guerard Heyward, Guerard Heyward's parents

Jacob Guerard Heyward (Guerard), eldest of the twelve children of George and Elizabeth Martha Heyward; married Pauline DeCaradeuc in 1866

Elise Heyward (Sister), eldest child of Pauline and Guerard Heyward

Margaret Heyward (Maude), daughter of Pauline and Guerard; named for Pauline's sister

Pauline Heyward (Nina), daughter of Pauline and Guerard

Jacob Guerard Heyward (Jack), first son born to Pauline and Guerard; died at age five

Frank Heyward, second son born to Pauline and Guerard

Walter Heyward, third son born to Pauline and Guerard

Pauline and Rose Heyward, twin daughters of Pauline and Guerard, died in infancy, as did Ethel Heyward

Friends

Carrie Griswold, Pauline's close friend, living with her mother and aunt at Montmorenci as refugees of the war

Margaret Heyward (Meta), cousin of Guerard Heyward, a close friend of Pauline's living in Aiken

Thomas Josias Heyward (Tom), Meta Heyward's brother

Mr. and Mrs. Jonathan Thomas Heyward, parents of Meta and Tom Heyward, and also friends of the DeCaradeuc family

Nellie and Mel Redmond, friends of Pauline, living in Berzelia, Georgia, near Augusta

Lizzie Coffin, friend of Pauline, living in Aiken

Amo Coffin, brother of Lizzie, Pauline's friend and former suitor

Dr. and Mrs. Amory Coffin of Aiken, parents of Lizzie, Amo, Charles and Frank; Dr. Coffin was the DeCaradeuc family physician

Julia, Fannie, Flint, and William Parrott, friends of the DeCaradeuc sisters in Aiken

Mary Farley, sister of W. D. and Hugh L. Farley, soldier friends of Pauline's brothers; lived in Laurensville, South Carolina

Robert M. (Robbie) and Phoebe C. Gibbes lived with their widowed mother in Graniteville, South Carolina

George Lalane, CSA lieutenant and suitor of Pauline's; died of wounds received in the Virginia campaigns in May 1864

John H. Cochran, CSA private and suitor of Pauline's; killed near Petersburg, Virginia, in July 1864

Mrs. A. M. McChesney, Augusta County, Virginia, mother of John H. Cochran; nursed Pauline's brother Frank during his fatal illness

Rosa Elmore and her cousins, Albert and Frank Elmore, friends of Pauline in Columbia

Servants at Montmorenci

| Jabe | Solomon |
| Joe | William |

A Confederate Lady Comes of Age

Prologue

Pauline DeCaradeuc Heyward (1843–1914) made the first entry in her journal on June 2, 1863, at Montmorenci, her family home near Aiken, South Carolina. She began when she was nineteen years old to record the day-to-day events of the Civil War from the perspective of a young southern woman utterly devoted to the rightness of the "Southern Cause." The deaths of her two soldier brothers had only served to strengthen her allegiance to the Confederacy and President Jefferson Davis. Throughout the war years Pauline remained a loyal Southerner, undaunted by invading Federal troops bent on punishing South Carolina for precipitating the war.

Pauline's journal, however, not only chronicles events of the war and her comments about them but also affords an intimate view of the dichotomous existence of southern families on the homefront struggling to preserve their social structure in the face of danger, deprivation, and decimation. Pauline was a pretty, well-educated, and spirited young woman who struggled to fulfill the expectations for women of nineteenth-century southern society while confronted with a war that would finally destroy the foundations of that society. She wavered between the youthful enjoyment of being the "belle of the ball" and outright contempt for social frivolity in the face of Confederate defeat. She longed for an end to the war and a normalization of her life, which included romance and ultimately marriage. In this respect she was not unlike many young southern women of her class who came of age during the hardship and tragedy of the Civil War.

Although her entries are intermittent, Pauline DeCaradeuc Heyward's journal spans a quarter of a century (1863–1888), which enables the reader to observe her transition from girlhood to mature womanhood. Over the years her journal became her friend and confidante, the recipient of thoughts and feelings deemed too private to share with anyone else: "My heart most usually bleeds inwardly, and this Journal is the only thing in this world that ever gets a peep into it. . . . Many and many is the thought coming from my inmost soul, which I have locked up here." The reader

1

thus comes to know Pauline DeCaradeuc Heyward in a very personal way, first as a nineteen year old striving to cope on the beleaguered South Carolina homefront during the Civil War and then as a young bride during the hardships and deprivation of the postwar Reconstruction South. In her later entries we see Pauline as a young mother and still later as an affluent matron.

Pauline's family background was that of affluence, education, and culture, which played a key role in shaping her life. Certainly the impact of the Civil War and Reconstruction molded her, but what was perhaps the most significant and steadfast influence in her life was her devout Catholicism. To be a Catholic in the mid-nineteenth-century South was to be out of the mainstream of society and part of a distinct minority in South Carolina.

The impression of Pauline DeCaradeuc Heyward that emerges from the pages of her journal is that of an intelligent and cultured young woman who, within the confines of the southern patriarchal society of her day, faced hardships and tragedies with courage, resourcefulness, and determination. To understand what made Pauline special and unique, one must understand her life within the context of her rather unusual family background; where she lived; the era in which she lived; as well as the events which influenced her life. To read her journal is to become intimately acquainted with a spirited southern woman who lived over one hundred years ago.

Pauline DeCaradeuc Heyward's Southern roots date back to 1792, when her paternal great-grandfather, General Jean Baptiste DeCaradeuc, arrived with his family in Charleston, South Carolina, as refugees from Santo Domingo. General DeCaradeuc owned several large sugar plantations in Santo Domingo, as had his father and grandfather before him. He was Commandant General de la Garde Nationale de Santo Domingo at the time of the slave uprising there. The insurrection, however, was not the reason for the general's flight from the island to Charleston in 1792. His departure was, rather, prompted by the arrival of French Republican commissioners from France who threatened to kill or send to the guillotine in Paris the "Aristocrate Commandant General."[1]

Jean Baptiste DeCaradeuc left Santo Domingo with his two sons, his daughter, and his widowed sister, Marie Louise

---

1. DeCaradeuc Papers 207, GHS: Journal and Genealogical Notes of Achille DeCaradeuc.

Chateaublond. His wife, Louise Agathe de la Toison Rocheblanche, had died there two years earlier. General DeCaradeuc and his family landed safely in Charleston, bringing with them a few slaves, many valuables, and a cargo of sugar. He was well situated in Charleston, and in a few years bought the Cedar Hill plantation in St. Thomas Parish, Charleston District, where in 1797 he built a home for his family.[2]

General DeCaradeuc died in 1810 at the age of sixty-eight and is buried in the family plot of the "Brick" Church (the St. Thomas and St. Denis Church) along the Clements Ferry Road, near Cedar Hill.[3] His only remaining heir was his son, Jean Baptiste Ursule Laurent (Hercule), Pauline's grandfather. In the year of his father's death Hercule married Marie Augustine Rossignol (Maxime) Lachicotte in St. Mary's Church in Charleston. Maxime as a young girl had also emigrated from Santo Domingo. Hercule and Maxime made their large Cedar Hill home a haven for refugees who fled from Santo Domingo and France. Hercule farmed, made bricks, and cut lumber on the plantation with the help of twenty slaves who had come from one of his father's sugar cane plantations in Santo Domingo. In 1813 Hercule and Maxime had a son, who died in infancy. Two years later John Baptiste DeCaradeuc was born, and in 1816 Maxime gave birth to Pauline's father, James Achille DeCaradeuc.[4]

The marriage ended tragically on November 18, 1820, when Hercule died of injuries sustained in a hunting accident.[5] In 1826 Maxime decided to return to France, where she had family, to rear and educate her two sons, John, age eleven, and Achille, age nine. The young widow rented the Cedar Hill plantation to her

---

2. General DeCaradeuc's decision to establish roots in South Carolina may well have been influenced by letters from Santo Domingo telling of the conditions there. A letter dated 1796 from his overseer, Mr. Jure, stated: "All your buildings, your Pottery, all your pavillons are burnt. Very few negro houses are left. It would be difficult to find cane plantings: the few negroes who remain only plant provisions." And later, in 1802, his brother, Caradeuc La Caye, wrote: "The Colony has never been in such a miserable condition. Remain where you are. The tribunals have rendered justice until 1802." (Letters cited in Journal of Achille DeCaradeuc.)
3. Robert F. Clute, "The Annals and Parish Register of St. Thomas and St. Denis Parish . . . ," SCHS File 20–40.
4. DeCaradeuc Papers 207, GHS: Sketch by Achille DeCaradeuc.
5. Elizabeth Heyward Jervey, "From Marriage and Death Notices from the City Gazette of Charleston, S.C.," *The South Carolina Historical and Genealogical Magazine* 48, 1947, p. 77.

brother and journeyed to Paris, where she was warmly received by her cousin Pauline Drouet, who was to become her lifelong friend. With the assistance of her cousin Maxime moved into an apartment and selected a school nearby for her young sons. Soon after, she received word that a "Conceil de Famille" had decided that the grandsons of General Jean Baptiste DeCaradeuc would have to be placed in a proper boarding school to be selected by the family council. The dauntless young widow indignantly replied that it was no business of theirs and that she would keep her sons with her.[6] The matter was laid to rest when she produced a copy of Hercule's will, which made her sole guardian of their children.

In 1829 Achille and John were sent to study mathematics under the tutelage of a Professor Guerard in order to prepare for admission to the Ecole Polytechnique. Professor Guerard, a graduate of that famous institution, took only ten young men at a time for study, accepting only the sons of the most prominent French families. Achille and John's fellow scholars included the Duc de Chartres, Ferdinand Philippe (1810–1842), and the Duc de Nemours, Louis Charles (1814–1896), sons of Louis Philippe (1773–1850), then Duc d'Orleans, who became "Citizen King" of the French in 1830, following the July Revolution against Charles X (1824–1830). John DeCaradeuc's closest friend was his classmate Edgar Ney (1812–1822), son of Napoleon's Marshal Michel Ney (1759–1815).[7] The plague of cholera which broke out in Europe in 1832 cut short the plans of Achille and John to enter the Ecole Polytechnique. When the death toll in Paris had reached one thousand a day, Maxime DeCaradeuc and her sons were persuaded by their relatives in Paris to leave France as soon as possible and return to South Carolina.

When Maxime left America in 1826, she took a trunk containing papers that had been saved by her father-in-law, General DeCaradeuc. Among his papers were plantation journals, letters, and documents concerning declarations for taxes. These papers enabled Maxime's lawyers to establish her right to a large amount in her claim against the French government for indemnities

---

6. DeCaradeuc Papers 207, GHS: Sketch by Achille DeCaradeuc. Achille noted that this incident occurred during the reign of Charles X, when much of the old regime prevailed. In former times family councils were all powerful where the sons of noble families were concerned.
7. *Ibid.*

regarding property losses sustained by the general in Santo Domingo. Maxime's astuteness enabled the family to collect an amount equal to about one-half the value of the Santo Domingo holdings. It was sufficient to support Maxime and her sons while they were in Paris, and to enable them to purchase property in South Carolina upon their return to America.

Tragedy again struck the DeCaradeuc family when John Baptiste died, unmarried, on November 11, 1836, at age twenty-two. Achille became the DeCaradeuc heir and, with his mother's help, purchased on February 21, 1840, for the sum of $2,000 a tract of land known as Conway's Valley. This property, containing "four hundred and thirty-seven acres more or less," was located seven miles from Aiken on the headwaters of Cedar Creek in Barnwell District, South Carolina.[8] Achille changed the name of the property to the Vale of Montmorenci because of the connection between the noted family of that name and the DeCaradeuc family of Bretagne.[9]

Nine months later, on November 12, 1840, Achille De-Caradeuc and Elizabeth Ann della Torre, daughter of Antonio and Margaret Ann Ryan della Torre, were married by Bishop John England at St. John's Catholic Church in Charleston.[10] Elizabeth Ann della Torre, who was born in Charleston on October 22, 1819, had prior to her marriage attended the Academy of Mme Ann Manson Talvande, a French emigrant from Santo Domingo.[11]

Achille DeCaradeuc and his twenty-one-year-old bride set up housekeeping in Charleston until a suitable home could be built

8. Copy of deed, courtesy of Mary DeCaradeuc Bartholomew. The town of Aiken had been founded in 1835 as a result of the routing of the 136-mile Charleston–Hamburg line constructed in 1833, the longest railroad in the world at that time. During the summer months Aiken became a popular resort for low country residents and during the war a place of refuge for many in the Charleston area threatened by Federal bombardment of coastal South Carolina.
9. DeCaradeuc Papers 1497, SHC: "Tribute to James Achille and Elizabeth Ann DeCaradeuc," by Thomas della Torre.
10. Pauline's maternal grandfather, Antonio della Torre, an Italian immigrant, had come to Charleston in 1809 and was a prosperous lumber merchant and owner of a steam sawmill. "From Schirmer Diary" (Jacob Frederic Schirmer, 1803–1880), *The South Carolina Historical Magazine*, 70, 1, 1969, p. 62.
11. *Ibid.*, 40, 1939, p. 16. Mabel L. Webber, "Copy of Some Loose Pages Found Among the Manigault Papers, in the Handwriting of Dr. Gabriel Manigault, Oct. 25, 1888"; DeCaradeuc Papers 1497, SHC: "Tribute. . . ." Elizabeth Ann della Torre's siblings were equally well educated and cultured individuals who pursued careers in law, business, education, and art.

on his newly acquired property near Aiken. It was in Charleston that Pauline was born on October 31, 1843. Pauline spent her early childhood in Charleston surrounded by art and learning. Her uncle John della Torre was an educator; her aunt Rose della Torre was an artist and art teacher; and her father was a talented miniaturist. Pauline later studied art, literature, history, French, and music, excelling in the latter.

When construction of the large house was completed, Achille moved his family into their new home, which he named Montmorenci.[12] There he became a pioneer in the cultivation of grapes and in the production of domestic wines, as well as a local authority on the subject.[13] He had imported French *vignerons* to work in his vineyards. In addition to these experienced laborers he had twenty-one slaves to further the farming and lumber interests of his estate. In the 1860 U.S. census Achille is listed as a lumber factor with real estate valued at $42,000 and a personal estate valued at $26,300. The DeCaradeuc family residing at Montmorenci at this time consisted of Achille's mother, Maxime; Achille and Elizabeth Ann; and their children, Frank, age nineteen, Pauline, sixteen, Antonio, fourteen, Margaret Ann, ten, and St. Julien, five.

It was here at Montmorenci that Pauline began keeping her journal in 1863. The year before, the DeCaradeuc family had suffered the loss of their two soldier sons, Frank and Antonio, and were trying their best to bring some degree of normalcy to the lives of those who remained at home. Pauline was deeply grieved over the death of her older brother, Frank. "Sometimes I wish I never had such a friend as Brother, one on whom my heart depended, & my life so linked, & then I never would have suffered so keenly in giving him up. . . ." It was for Pauline's sake that her parents invited her friend Carrie Griswold to live with them for

---

12. In a diary entry dated Monday, July 27, 1846, the Rev. John Hamilton Cornish gives the following description of the Montmorenci estate: "About six miles east of Aiken brought us to Mr. Caradeaux's who has a beautiful farm in a valley between ledges of rocks, which he calls 'Mount Morency'—his house is on the side hill, a sweet spring of water close by it. He has an abundance of apples, peaches and various kinds of fruits—has something of a vineyard planted, plenty and a large variety of grapes." John Hamilton Cornish Papers 1461, SHC.

13. *Ibid.,* Cornish diary entry dated Thursday, October 7, 1858: "Attended the meeting of the Aiken Fruit Growing and Horticultural Society. A very interesting report by Mr. DeCaradeaux on the culture of the grape."

the duration of the war. In spite of acute shortages of food, clothing, and other necessities, the family generously opened their home to Confederate soldiers and war refugees. Visits were made and visits were paid in the face of a constant threat of invasion by Federal forces. Pauline frequently rode the train ("the cars") to Aiken and to Augusta, Georgia, to visit friends. She also made extended trips by rail to Charleston, Columbia, and Savannah, usually in the company of an older family member or friend.

As the war continued to grind on relentlessly, news from the battlefront became more and more grievous to those at home. The dreaded lists of South Carolina soldiers killed or wounded in the Virginia campaigns were released with alarming frequency. Pauline's grief over the loss of her brothers was compounded by the deaths of two friends and suitors: George Lalane in May 1864 in the Wilderness campaign, and John H. Cochran in July 1864 in the trenches at Petersburg. Many other young officers, friends of her brothers and acquaintances of Pauline, also died in the Virginia battles. Pauline's sadness and unhappiness are palpable as she faces the loss of those near and dear to her. "I have no heart to keep this Journal or tell of the dreadful, fatal battles in Va. Oh my God! my heart is too heavy, I am entirely miserable."

The women of the DeCaradeuc household displayed great courage and resourcefulness in the face of wartime threats and dangers. When General Kilpatrick's troops arrived at Montmorenci in February of 1865, during Achille's absence, Pauline's mother and grandmother faced the intruders alone and attempted to thwart the invasion of their home—to no avail. They did, however, succeed in saving Montmorenci from being put to the torch. Later it was young Pauline who bravely journeyed to Augusta to demand a protective guard from General Molineux, commander of the Federal garrison in Augusta, following repeated intrusions suffered by the DeCaradeuc family from marauding soldiers in the Aiken area.

Pauline, an unusually pretty young woman with dark eyes and dark hair, was very popular at social functions. Nevertheless, she was frequently troubled and dissatisfied. "I should have enjoyed it very, very much, but this unaccountable something buried in my heart worries me so. . . ." "If kind and plentiful attention, & admiration could have influenced me, I should have been better, for I received a great deal of it in Savannah, but *that* is *not* what I want. . . ." She was a literate and talented young woman whose formal education was, in all likelihood, obtained under the tutelage of Catholic nuns. During the war years at Montmorenci Pauline continued to study French diligently; she read Shakespeare and history daily; and she tutored her young brother, St. Julien, and his friend Frank Coffin for several hours each day. In addition, she loved poetry, art, and music, and was an accomplished pianist who played frequently on social occasions.

Pauline DeCaradeuc Heyward's ethnic background was French Catholic, Irish Catholic, and Italian Catholic, and her family was prominent among the few Catholic families in the Aiken area.[14] Because of their culture and learning the DeCaradeuc family was accepted socially by the upper-class Protestants residing in the area. Pauline had many friends and beaux but in spite of her popularity remained dissatisfied. "Why do I always inspire *general* admiration, it is the same thing every where I go, I would much rather, a great deal have but one or two admirers at a party, &c., and let them be agreeable and devoted, instead of having a little bit of *everybody's* attention. I consider myself very unfortunate in this respect." To some of her young suitors Pauline's religion posed no problem, but to others it did. Young Amo Coffin had loved Pauline for some time, and it was believed by her intimates that it was the great differences in their religious faiths that kept them from "being a match."[15] Pauline was aware of the problems created by her devotion to Catholicism and made note of this fact in her journal: "My faith has kept back a good many from seriousness; John Milledge last summer couldn't abide it, & this only increases my ardent love for it." Young Guerard Heyward, however, persevered in his courtship of Pauline in spite of their religious differences.

---

14. There was no Catholic church in Aiken until one was erected in 1867 by Bishop Ignatio Persico, a close friend of the family. Bishop Persico stayed at Montmorenci on a number of occasions, as did mission priests. Since Augusta, Georgia, was only 17 miles from Aiken and rail service took only an hour, Pauline and other family members frequently rode the cars to Augusta to attend mass on holy days at the Most Holy Trinity Church. J. J. O'Connell, O.S.B., *Catholicity in the Carolinas and Georgia: Leaves of Its History*, 1879; rpt. 1972, pp. 183, 554–555; *History of Saint Mary Help of Christians Church and the Aiken Missions*, 1867–1942, p. 30; Derrick, *Centennial History of the South Carolina Railroad*, p. 211.
15. Amo Coffin was the son of Dr. and Mrs. Amory Coffin, prominent members of St. Thaddeus' Episcopal Church in Aiken, whose rector was the Rev. John Hamilton Cornish.

Pauline met Guerard Heyward (1844–1888) in August of 1865 while attending a dinner party given by a neighbor, Mr. L. S. Benson. Guerard, a graduate of the South Carolina Military Academy (The Citadel), had served as an officer in the First South Carolina Artillery. He had recently been released from a Federal prison where he had spent the last two years of the war, having been wounded and taken prisoner in July of 1863.

Guerard Heyward's family also had roots deeply embedded in the South Carolina soil. His great-grandfather was Thomas Heyward (1746–1809), one of the four South Carolina signers of the Declaration of Independence. Guerard's father, George Cuthbert Heyward (1822–1867), was born in Beaufort County at Bluff Plantation, where he continued to live with his widowed mother for many years.[16] In the decade prior to the Civil War, Guerard's father moved to Charleston, where he went into business as a commission merchant.[17] When hostilities began, Guerard and his father enlisted in the South Carolina military forces.[18] George Heyward moved his large family from Charleston to Aiken, where they resided during the war.

Following a courtship of several months Pauline happily confided in her journal her love for Guerard: "I am engaged to be married, in love, at last, yes positively & terribly in love. . . ." Concerning the engagement of Pauline and Guerard, the Rev. John H. Cornish, in a diary entry dated October 23, 1865, made this comment: "On the cars returning [from Augusta to Aiken] were Guerard Heyward and Miss Pauline DeCaradeuc to whom he has recently become engaged. There seems to be no objection on the part of his parents, but one, which is a serious one. She is a very devout Roman Catholic, otherwise one would say they are happily mated."[19]

16. In the 1850 U.S. Census, George C. Heyward, planter, and his wife, Elizabeth (Guerard) Heyward, and five children are listed in St. Helena Parish, Town of Beaufort.
17. G. C. Heyward (DeVeaux & Heyward), commission merchant, Vanderhorst's wharf, h. Coming; *The Charleston City Directory,* 1859, p. 94.
18. Guerard, age 17, received a lieutenancy in the First South Carolina Regulars and participated in the bombardment of Ft. Sumter. George C. Heyward received a captaincy in the Third South Carolina Cavalry.
19. Cornish Papers 1461, SHC. The George C. Heyward family were members of St. Thaddeus' Episcopal Church.

The DeCaradeucs were a closely knit and loving family, and Pauline's journal entries reveal her devotion to her family, especially to her mother and beloved "Fa." Although in straitened circumstances after the war, her parents would make many sacrifices to give her a proper wedding. ". . . more devoted, loving, unselfish and self-abnegating parents never lived. I feel that I never, never can love and cherish them sufficiently to return their utter devotion to me. . . ."

Pauline's entries at this time reflected an ambivalent attitude toward marriage not uncommon among young southern women of her class. Pauline repeatedly expressed a desire to postpone her wedding date. Her seeming contrariness, however, was not due to a lack of commitment to marry Guerard Heyward, but was simply a reluctance on her part to end the courtship period. "I know I can't help being *entirely* happy when I'll be with him forever and bear his name, and yet, you know, I don't want to be married—I am, Oh! *so* happy *now*." Pauline well knew that marriage brought with it the responsibilities of being a wife, a mother, and the mistress of her own household. It also meant separation from her beloved family and an end to the freedoms enjoyed in her father's home.

Pauline finally yielded to Guerard's gentle persistence, and on November 6, 1866, the young couple were joined in holy matrimony by the Catholic Bishop Patrick N. Lynch, at Montmorenci.[20] After a brief trip to Charleston to visit Guerard's family, the newlyweds moved to their own home in the small town of Bluffton, where Guerard was engaged in planting.

The war had taken a heavy toll on both the DeCaradeuc and Heyward families, leaving them in greatly reduced circumstances. The ravages of war brought an end to Achille DeCaradeuc's work in viticulture and viniculture. His vineyards had been destroyed and the land laid waste. Ironically, during the difficult period of Reconstruction in South Carolina the DeCaradeuc family was aided by payments from the French government as compensation for the 1792 emancipation of the Santo Domingo slaves of Achille's grandfather, General Jean Baptiste DeCaradeuc.[21] Following an

---

20. Throughout their marriage religious differences were never a major problem. Pauline remained devoutly Catholic and reared her children in her faith. Guerard never converted to Catholicism; the Rev. Charles H. Strong, rector of St. John's Episcopal Church, Savannah, officiated at his funeral service.
21. DeCaradeuc Papers 1497, SHC: "Tribute . . . ."

unsuccessful effort to plant cotton on his land, Achille DeCaradeuc, whose former classmates included the sons of the king of France, was forced to take a job as chief engineer and land agent of the South Carolina Railroad. In 1869 he moved back to Charleston, where he rented a home.[22] Montmorenci was sold to Augustus A. Ruxton for the sum of $10,000 on February 28, 1870.[23]

Guerard's family fared little better. In October of 1865, Captain George Cuthbert Heyward moved his family from Aiken back to Charleston.[24] After a brief stay they returned to Beaufort County and settled in Bluffton, near Guerard and Pauline. There Captain Heyward and his older sons planted in an attempt to recover from the substantial losses they suffered during the Civil War.

Young Guerard found planting neither profitable nor satisfying, so in 1869 he obtained a job as a bookkeeper in Savannah, Georgia. Pauline and Guerard moved to Savannah, where they lived for the rest of their lives. During their marriage of a little over twenty years they had nine children, five of whom survived childhood. Pauline was a devoted wife, centering her life around her husband and children. In 1876 Guerard, an astute businessman, became a partner in H. M. Comer & Co., a prosperous Savannah cotton and rice factoring firm.[25] The family enjoyed a comfortable life style until 1888, when Guerard died suddenly at the age of forty-four.

Pauline was so devastated by Guerard's death that she ended her journal of twenty-five years on the date of his demise with the emotionally terse entry: "FINIS. March 5, 1888."

But life was not over for Pauline DeCaradeuc Heyward. She now had the sole responsibility of rearing and providing for her surviving five children. She faced the loss of her husband and the hardships that followed with the same resourcefulness, courage, and faith which had sustained her throughout her life.

---

22. *Ibid.*, Memoir of Achille DeCaradeuc.
23. Copy of bill of sale, courtesy of Mary DeCaradeuc Bartholomew.
24. Cornish Papers, diary entry of October 23, 1865.
25. *Sholes' Savannah Directory, 1880*, p. 232; obituary, *Savannah Morning News,* Mar. 6, 1888.

The Journal of
Pauline
DeCaradeuc Heyward

1863

Chapter One

The Wages of War: "Silent Graves," Winchester, and Vicksburg

Tuesday, June 2, 1863

The tidings from Vicksburg continue favorable, so far, but the struggles for it are desperate on both sides. Grant, the Yankee Gen. in command, has outgeneraled Pemberton, but if Johnston has *only* been sent in time, he'll find more than his match there, as Johnston is universally believed to be our greatest General, not excepting even Lee; however, Lee has *never* lost a battle; give me that kind of a man for my Hero General.[1] Ewell has taken poor Stonewall's command.[2] I heard a very characteristic anecdote of our glorious Stonewall; he was conversing with one of his aides, and in the course of conversation said, that there was one thing which of all others he liked most and that was brandy and water! "Why," said the Officer, "how is it that I've never seen you touch it." "No," said Jackson, "neither you nor any other man has ever seen me taste it for fifteen years, it is because of my passion

---

1. Following the bloody and costly engagement at Champion's Hill on May 16, 1863, resulting in 2,441 Federal casualties and 3,851 Confederate casualties, Lt. Gen. John C. Pemberton, CSA, made the fateful decision to fall back to Vicksburg. On May 18 the siege of Vicksburg began. Gen. Ulysses S. Grant's efforts to avoid a long siege by quickly mounting two assaults met with failure and severe losses: 3,199 Federal casualties, with Confederate losses less than 500. In an effort to relieve Pemberton, Confederate troops were being assembled in Jackson, Mississippi, under the command of Gen Joseph E. Johnston, the department commander, and at this time numbered around 6,000. *OR*, I, 24, pt. 2, pp. 399–418; Hattaway and Jones, *How the North Won: A Military History of the Civil War*, 1983, pp. 375–412; Deming, *The Life of Ulysses S. Grant, U.S. Army*, 1868, pp. 209–59.
2. Lt. Gen. Richard S. Ewell replaced Lt. Gen. Thomas J. (Stonewall) Jackson, who died, May 9, 1863, the result of wounds received May 2 at Chancellorsville when his own men mistook his reconnoitering party for Federal cavalry.

for it that I never taste it." This is illustrative of that wonderful degree of self-abnegation and command which was so noble in him.

Uncle John[3] dined with us yesterday and remained all night on account of the rain; he looks dreadfully since his illness. I do believe I admire and love him more every time I see him.

Mr. and Mrs. Walker[4] spent the evening with us. I heard from Harriott [Toomer], she is full of gaiety and writes me of all the "fun" she is having in Charleston, it all grates harshly on my heart now! and I don't know how any one can feel so bright and happy now and even feeling so, how they can write those feelings to me, whose heart is so wretched and sorrowful as mine.

Harriott Toomer has been constantly writing to me about Lieut. George Lalane,[5] that he hadn't forgotten his old "sweetheart" and was coming to see me, etc. I never paid any attention to her remarks, knowing Cordes [Boylston] to be her authority. C. sent me word that G.L. was on his way to see me on important business! Of course, I didn't notice his messages, he [Cordes] is too stupid.

Well, I went to Augusta and in passing the hotel a young soldier sprang up from a seat, and ran towards me with both hands extended, as if he wanted to shake both hands, he looked very glad to see me indeed, but I did not know him, and when he reached me, with a hearty ejaculation of "Good Gracious!" I drew back saying, "Excuse me, Sir, you mistake me for someone else." Bowed and passed on; when I reached the corner, I remembered his features as Lalane's, I turned but he was gone, nor did I again see him, 'tho I intentionally passed the hotel three times again. Harriott writes me that he was there on his way to see me, and reproaches me for treating him so badly. He wishes he never had left Virginia. But how can I help it? I'll wait patiently for the next step whatever it may be.

3. John C. della Torre, Pauline's maternal uncle, was a teacher and administrative assistant at the High School of Charleston.
4. Probably a reference to Mr. and Mrs. William Walker, who lived near Aiken.
5. Second Lt. George M. Lalane, Company E, 25th Regiment (Infantry), South Carolina Volunteers. Salley, *South Carolina Troops in Confederate Service*, 2, 1914, p. 231.

June 11, 1863

I woke up this morning from the happiest dream I ever had. I was in our old home [Charleston] where we were all so happy, and I was sitting on Mother's room steps. I looked up and saw my darling, precious Brother, crossing the yard. I sprang down to meet him and he caught me in his dear arms; he had come home from the wars and there was peace. I felt him kissing me over and over and we were both weeping, because we were thinking of our dearest pet and pride Tonio, and I woke up saying, "Thank God, Brother, that 'tho our darling is dead, I still have you." Oh, how distinctly I felt his tears on my cheek and his arms around me, and how happy, Oh! *how happy I was.* Ah! my own dearest Brother, the thought is killing to me, that I am *never, never* to see you again or feel those precious arms about me, except in my dreams, those empty dreams. Oh! my God, my life is such a blank, dreary thing without my Brother. I am so lonely and lost without him.[6]

June 12, 1863

I went out to Johnston's[7] this afternoon for the mail, on horseback, while there I saw a most superb black horse, come up; the servant who was riding, could with difficulty manage him. He had cavalry trappings. I was admiring the magnificent animal very much when Nellie Cumber told me 'twas young Hankinson's horse, that he had just returned from Virginia and brought his horse. My God! what a rush came over my heart, 'twas Brother's horse, "Sidney Johnston." The horse Fa gave him the day before he left for Virginia and of which he was so proud and fond. His Company wouldn't consent, or, rather the authorities wouldn't allow either Brother's or Tonio's horses to leave Va. and they were sold there. Hankinson bought Brother's, I never saw it before.

6. Lieutenant François DeCaradeuc, a member of Col. J. L. Black's First Regiment of South Carolina Cavalry—Pauline's beloved brother Frank—was born October 24, 1841, in Charleston and died December 2, 1862, in Staunton, Virginia, of typhoid pneumonia. John Antonio DeCaradeuc (Tonio) was born in 1845 in Charleston and died November 3, 1862, in Richmond, predeceasing his older brother by only one month. Tonio also served in Black's First. DeCaradeuc Papers 1497, SHC: Memoir . . . .
7. Johnston's station was 5 miles north of Aiken.

Ah! my heart almost broke as I rode home contrasting our home with the Hankinson's. There he had come home well and happy, what joy to shed over his home, I know best, too well. His mother, father and sisters will go out with him to see his beautiful horse— My Brother's horse—they will caress it to please him, and look on with such pride and delight, as he mounts it and manoeuvres to display its graces and beauty for them. And, Oh! all he'll have to tell them, how joyously they'll cling round him to hear. What happiness he has brought them all. While our home! Two silent sad graves in the garden, two silent hats and spurs hanging in the entry, is all that is to fill our hearts and Oh! God, for the *too, too* happy hearts that would have been round him, and now to think, he is *dead, silent, forever,* while others, Oh! *so far* his inferiors in *everything,* live and take his place. That those graves in the garden is all that is left of our brave boys, while others will come home to bring such bliss. Ah! I only realize this greatest trial when I see others return home glad and well, and none come to us, ours (I only feel it then)—have come for the last time.

The Yankees crossed the Rappahanock into several places. At five o'clock on the 11th of June the battle was fought at Winchester, Va., lasted till five P.M., when Gen. Stuart obliged them to recross. All quiet at Vicksburg. The battle was a bloody one, and the attack by the enemy was unexpected. 'Twas a hand to hand fight most of the time, first large Cavalry fight, yet, mounted foe numbered 8 or 10,000, accompanied by 2 or 3,000 dismounted men and artillery.[8] The garrison at both Vicksburg and Fort Hudson were really starving when they surrendered, at

---

8. On June 9, 1863, Maj. Gen. Alfred Pleasonton's Federal cavalry crossed the Rappahannock River and surprised Maj. Gen. J. E. B. Stuart's cavalrymen. At Brandy Station, Virginia, there ensued a fierce fight, considered the largest cavalry engagement of the war. Union losses numbered 936 and Confederate losses 523. Clement Evans, ed., *CMH*, 3, 1899, rpr. 1962, pp. 396–97; Patricia L. Faust, ed., *Historical Times Illustrated Encyclopedia of The Civil War*, 1986, p. 76.

In the Second Battle of Winchester, June 13–15, 1863, the Second Corps under the command of Lt. Gen. Richard Ewell cleared from the Shenandoah Valley a Federal garrison of some 6,000 men under the command of Maj. Gen. Robert H. Milroy. Federal losses totaled 4,443; Confederate losses 252. *OR*, I, 27, pt. 2, pp. 53, 335–36, 459–64.

both places the last pound of mule flesh and last grain of peas were eaten by the suffering inmates.[9]

July 26 [1863]

Clara Gregg came down in the beginning of the week and remained 'til today. When I went out to put her on the train, just after she got in, her sweetheart jumped out, he bowed to me and went into another car, I am afraid they didn't see each other. Clara is not nearly as youthful or gay in her manner as formerly, and she thinks we'll all be old maids yet, I don't doubt it, neither do I care very much.[10]

August 1, 1863

My dear Ma[11] has been desperately ill, on the brink of death, we have been staying with her for several days, she has now rallied, it is over a year now, since she has been confined to bed, with the most cruel and painful disease during which time, not one murmer has escaped her lips, not even to say she was tired, but even in her agony, her sweet smile and cheerful, *christian* word is there for *all*. I never expect to see such a Holy Christian again.

Uncle John looks dreadfully, I fear consumption has marked him for her prey; then what will become of his little family? and

---

9. The siege of Vicksburg began May 18, 1863, and ended July 4, 1863, with the surrender of the city by Lt. Gen. Pemberton to Gen. Ulysses S. Grant. Thus ended a prolonged period of constant bombardment and starvation for soldier and civilian alike. Mule meat had indeed become a luxury in the besieged city. In a letter to Maj. Gen. George Henry Thomas, July 11, 1863, Grant stated that among the spoils were 30,000 rebel troops, and that 60,000 Confederates had been wounded, captured, and scattered during the siege.

On July 8 Port Hudson, Louisiana, fell, and the Federal forces gained control of the entire Mississippi River. Deming, *Grant*, pp. 260–97; *OR*, I, 24, pt. 1, pp. 36–62, 272–85.

10. Rosa Clara Gregg, daughter of Mr. and Mrs. William G. Gregg of Edgefield County, South Carolina, married Nathaniel G. R. Chafee, April 5, 1864, at Trinity Church in Columbia. SHC: Cornish Diary, Apr. 5, 1864.

11. Pauline's grandmother, Margaret Ann della Torre, widow of Antonio della Torre of Charleston.

what will we all do, Uncle John is the idol of the whole family, but surely God has stricken us as much as He will; and we pray night and day for mercy.

I heard from Mary Farley again, she begs me to tell her all I ever heard of the exploits of her brother, and write an account of his imprisonment,[12] as Mrs. de Fountaine wishes to write the biography of all who have distinguished themselves and been martyrs in the cause. I will do all I can towards helping her, and have already written to a young man in Va. who used to scout with him, to request him to write them for me. I must too, get together the adventures of my hero Brothers for the same purpose.

August 9, 1863

Mother received a long and very beautiful letter from that sweetest of women, Mrs. McChesney. Oh! if I only knew her personality! She who tended my beloved Brother with such angelic kindness, and kissed him while he was dying beneath her roof.[13] She says, in her letter, in speaking of me, "It seems too formal in speaking of her to put the prefix, Miss, I feel as tho I had known her and esteemed her, thro the introduction of her nobel angel brother, Frank, who loved her so much. Whenever I think of him, the loving and beloved sister is also brought to my mind. He talked of her so much before he became delirious, and in his wildest moments seemed ever anxious to see her and be with his dearest Paul."

Her letter is filled with recollections of my dearest Brother; he made a great impression on her. She says, "His educated mind and superior manner first attracted the Dr. and us towards him. It was only necessary to know him to love him for his patient goodness and Christian fortitude."

Oh! if I only could see her, to show her how much I love her!

12. First Lt. W. D. Farley, South Carolina Volunteers, captain on Gen. Milledge Luke Bonham's staff, was captured and imprisoned in November 1861 with Pauline's brother Frank. Farley was mortally wounded June 9, 1863, in the Gettysburg campaign. As a volunteer aide on the staff of Maj. Gen. J. E. B. Stuart he was praised by his commander as having served "without emolument, long, faithfully and always with distinction" (*OR*, I, 5, p. 449; *OR*, I, 27, pt. 2, pp. 684–85, 731).
13. Mrs. A. M. McChesney of Augusta County, Virginia, cared for Frank DeCaradeuc in her home during his final illness.

Chapter Two

Charleston Besieged: General Gillmore Shells a Sleeping City, Fort Sumter Holds Out

August 12th, 1863

The attack on Charleston, or rather Battery Wagner on Morris Island, is continued vigorously, but the Charlestonians seem determined to sacrifice everything—life, property, friends, before giving up.

God strengthen us in the determination.

Complaints of Beauregarde are made loud and deep thro'out the state and the "Mercury" [*Charleston Mercury*] is hotter against the administration then ever. This dissatisfaction, if as I believe—¹ is groundless—spreads an unfortunate influence over the country.[1]

Pemberton's army detest him, 'tis said and Price has resigned.[2] Things are dark enough. The *London Times,* thinks a 20-year war not impossible, it says fighting can never end the

---

1. Battery Wagner on Morris Island and Fort Sumter guarded the approaches to Charleston harbor. On July 10, 1863, the Federal forces under the command of Brig. Gen. Quincy A. Gillmore landed on the south end of Morris Island, capturing the Confederate fortified position there. In spite of the criticism directed toward Gen. Pierre G. T. Beauregard, CSA, who commanded the defenses of coastal Georgia and South Carolina, his army successfully turned back assaults on Battery Wagner, July 11 and 18, 1863. *OR,* I, 28, pt. 1, p. 5; Hattaway and Jones, pp. 426–27; Faust, pp. 51–52.
2. It was Lt. Gen. John C. Pemberton who resigned his high rank when no assignment could be found for him following the surrender of Vicksburg. He later accepted an appointment as a colonel of artillery.

   The reference to Maj. Gen. Sterling Price is perhaps related to his ongoing feud with Brig. Gen. Ben McCulloch. In spite of his defeats at Pea Ridge, Iuka, Corinth, and Helena, Price retained popularity with his men and respect from his enemies.

war! Then why in the name of all that's sensible don't they intervene?

I received a letter from Harriott [Toomer], her aunt Mrs. Cordes is dead, their troubles are just commencing.

August 22nd, 1863

The abolitionists are still besieging dear Charleston closely, 'tis thought that "Grim old Sumter" can't hold out much longer. Our forces on Morris Island are dependent on Charleston for provisions and water, the Yankees prevent our steamers from conveying it, by their shelling, so 'tis only carried at night by row boats. Bad, very bad! this.

We have removed all the guns from Sumter except the Barbette one; there are 400 negroes at work in it, fixing sand bags.

Battery Wagner is still "like the air invulnerable" and our troops hopeful; but the beseigers can be relieved and renewed at any time, while—alas! poor Charleston, I fear, I fear.[3]

Yesterday was appointed by Davis as a day of fasting and prayer. I fear our self-confidence, boasting and pride of the successes accorded us by God, have weighed heavily in the balance against the justice of our cause in the hand of our Creator, and these reverses and terrible humiliations, come from Him to humble our hearts and remind us of our total helplessness without His aid.

August 26th, 1863

Father went to Charleston on Sunday and returned today, the Yankees are shelling the City, they commenced shelling it at 2 o'clock A.M. on 21st August.

---

3. A barbette was a raised wooden platform or mound of earth which permitted artillery to be fired over the parapet without exposing the gun crew. These guns at Fort Sumter were delivering "accurate and destructive fire" over both Wagner and Gregg. Battery Wagner's defense, therefore, was enhanced by the firing from Fort Sumter as well as its own artillery and secure bombproof shelter, large enough for its entire garrison. Faust, pp. 38–39; OR I, 28, pt. 1, p. 16–17.

Gillmore sent warning to Beauregarde giving four hours time to remove non-combatants, but did not allow the message time to reach him before he began shelling the sleeping women and children.[4] God has preserved them, thus far no one has been injured. One shell went thro the roof of a house and straight thro the first floor, thro the wall of the entry into a room on the second floor tearing away the bed from under a little child (without hurting it) then going thro that floor into the basement and thro the brick wall of that, into the yard which was paved, and there buried itself six feet in the earth, scattering the bricks about with such force that some of them flew over the street & broke the door of the opposite house. Father saw this himself.

Fort Sumter still holds out, but must soon fall. The women and children have all left the City, Mrs. Martin and Mrs. Solee are here with us. Cordes Boylston is seriously injured. Whilst at dinner in [Fort] Sumter a shell fell on the table, wounding several [soldiers] & driving his [Cordes's] plate thro' cutting the knife he held, in half. A short time before part of his bed was torn from under him. Again he was on the point of shaking hands with another officer, when a shell fell between them, taking off four fingers of the officer.[5]

Last night the Yankees made two desperate attacks on our batteries at Morris Island, but were completely defeated each time. We have two guns, new ones, called Blakely guns, which reach 8 miles and the balls weigh 800 lbs. & shell 600 & something over, they were to reach town yesterday, trust they will help us well.

---

4. Brig. Gen. Quincy A. Gillmore demanded the immediate evacuation of Morris Island and Fort Sumter by the Confederate forces in a communication to Gen. Beauregard dated August 21, 1863. If compliance with the demand was not forthcoming or a reply received within four hours, Gillmore threatened to "open fire on the city of Charleston from batteries already established within easy and effective range of the heart of the city." The unsigned communication was delayed in reaching Beauregard, who replied August 22, 1863. In his reply Beauregard severely castigated Gillmore for "turning his guns against the old men, the women and children and the hospitals of a sleeping city" without allowing time for the evacuation of noncombatants. "This reckless course of action," Beauregard added, was "atrocious and unworthy of any soldier." *OR*, I, 28, pt. 2, pp. 57–59.

5. In a report of Col. Alfred Rhett, First South Carolina Artillery commanding Fort Sumter, operations August 12 to September 4, 1863, Lieutenant S. Cordes Boylston, adjutant, was reported seriously bruised by a shell bursting above the mess room, and later severely wounded in the back on August 23, 1863. *Ibid.*, pt. 1, pp. 615–16.

Father visited our cousin, young Morell,[6] who is ill in a hospital there with typhoid fever, he is alone there without any relatives near him, there are some things he is longing for, I intend sending him a box. I have some money which I can put to no better purpose, his case reminds me so much of darling, darling Tonio's, he is so young too, poor little fellow, I feel so much for him.

Sept. 4th, 1863

I spent four or five days at Rosemill [Rose Hill],[7] helping to move Ma & Daughter [Pauline's grandmother della Torre and great-aunt Eliza McDonald], returned & went to Augusta yesterday, met one or two acquaintances & came home very tired.

Sept. 12th, 1863

Morris Island has at last been carried by the foe, for three days & nights the enemy were firing upon our batteries there, with their tremendous Parrott & mortar guns, from their iron clads & batteries, so quickly too, it was the severest bombardment of the war, the bombproofs at Battery Wagner were bared by their shelling.

About six o'clock in the afternoon of Sept. 6th, 1863 our forces were withdrawn from the Island, the guns were double shotted, fired & spiked, etc., the evacuation conducted by Col. Rhett assisted by Maj. Bryan.

The enemy kept up a strong fire on our men, but only one barge, containing 12 men was lost, they commenced bombarding the Island on July 10th & only took it Sept. 6th.[8]

6. Probably a reference to Private John Morrell, Company G, 28th Georgia, who apparently survived his fever only to sustain a concussion from an exploding mortar shell November 7, 1863, at Fort Sumter. *Ibid.*, p. 635.
7. "Rosemill" represents an error in the transcription of the journal. The home referred to was Rose Hill, the home of Pauline's great-aunt and uncle, Dr. and Mrs. J.C.W. McDonald, located 6 miles from Montmorenci. Hereinafter all references to "Rosemill" will be emended to read "Rose Hill." DeCaradeuc Papers, 1497, SHC: "Tribute . . . ."
8. The attack on Morris Island began on July 10, 1863, when Federal forces succeeded in occupying the south end of the island. Following two unsuccessful assaults on Battery Wagner, on July 11 and 18, Federal forces instituted a

Fort Sumter is a mass of ruins, the South walls are completely destroyed and there is not a cannon there, Rhett &
command were removed a short time ago because artilleryists
were no longer needed there, and Maj. Blake commands, & with
his infantry, The Chston Battalion, occupys it. At 1 o'clock A.M.
on the 9th of Sept. a number of barges, 30 or 40 in number,
approached poor dilapidated Sumter, at a signal from the Fort,
the guns of Ft. Johnson, Battery Simkins, Ft. Moultrie & the
Chicora opened upon them, their musketry. The enemy soon,
however, reached the ledge & sprang to the assault. They were
met by men determined enough, who, after discharging their
muskets did not take time to reload but poured upon them such
torrents of brickbats from the ruins around, that the enemy could
not stand it. The men, in the barges terror stricken abandoned
the attack leaving their comrades who had landed, wholly without support, who surrendered. Thirteen (13) Yankee Naval officers
& 102 men, 3 stands of colors & four beautiful barges, was the
result of this performance & while we lost not a man. Among the
flags taken is one that waved over the fort in April, 1861, which
Anderson was allowed to carry North. Admiral [John A.] Dahlgren
had undertaken "to repossess the fort & restore the old Flag."[9]

siege which lasted from July 18 to September 7. Total Federal casualties
during the entire operation were 2,318. The total Confederate casualties numbered 990.

The evacuation of Morris Island took place on the night of September 6 under
the command of Col. Lawrence Keitt, not Col. Rhett as Pauline stated. Major
Henry Bryan, a member of Gen. Beauregard's staff, who had volunteered as
Keitt's adjutant general, played a key role in the success of the evacuation.
For a detailed description see Report of Col. Keitt, September 7, 1863. *OR*, I,
28, pt. 1, pp. 210, 408–9, 483–88.

9. Fort Sumter had been held by the First South Carolina Artillery under the
command of Col. Alfred Rhett. Brig. Gen. R. S. Ripley decided to replace the
artillerymen with infantrymen, and on the night of September 4 the Charleston Battalion under the command of Maj. Julius A. Blake relieved the garrison.
Col. Rhett assumed command of the interior batteries of Charleston, with
Castle Pinckney and Fort Ripley.

On September 9 a Federal force of 400 men attacked Fort Sumter and were
repulsed by 80 riflemen and 24 men armed with grenades, fireballs, and
masses of masonry. The Confederates captured 11 Federal officers and 110
men and reported 6 enemy killed and 15 wounded; they also seized 5 barges
and 5 stands of colors, one of which was reported to be the flag taken from Fort
Sumter by Maj. Robert Anderson when Confederate forces seized the fort in
1861. Numerous small arms and other accouterments were also reported seized.
No Confederate soldiers sustained injuries in the engagement. *Ibid.*, pp. 125,
400, 727.

Our casualties on Morris Island during the struggle of 48 days is estimated at 702 killed, wounded & missing, the enemy's 600. The enemy made three desperate attempts to carry our batteries on Morris Island by storm but were each time completely repulsed.

Sept. 20th, 1863

Well a great deal has happened since I wrote. I went home with Aunt Ada & Uncle John, a few days ago, to assist them in their preparations for going to Europe, dear Uncle John's life depends on it, 'tis the last alternative. They are to run the blockade from Wilmington. I helped Aunt Ada to secret their valuables, their exchange, etc. We made a quantity of secret pockets in the linings, hem & folds of her dress, where some of her jewels are, and then she has a flannel skirt made of a blanket, in the heavy folds are her diamonds sewed up. In the double leather of Uncle John's shoes are his diamond studs, & she has a bustle, & padding for her bosom, stuffed with pearls, etc. I made a black silk belt for her, in which is sewed up their exchange. God bless them, they went this morning, I went to the cars to see them pass by, for a final adieu.

Oh! I fear it *was* a final adieu to my dearest Uncle, his health is so fearfully bad. Their two little baby girls are left with us. Tante has Tom [Tommie della Torre].[10]

Nov. 19th, 1863

On the 6th I went to Charleston with Fa. & Tante, on business, how sad & strange to be there without Brother or Tonio, the old City is turned entirely into the military, so many private houses, long since vacated by the owners, are quarters for officers and converted into Pay master quarters, hospitals, commissary departments, etc.

We visited the fortifications on the battery and saw the two gun boats lying off in the Bay, a Regt. was encamped on the green

---

10. Tante was Pauline's Aunt Rose della Torre. Tom was Pauline's first cousin, the young son of John and Ada della Torre.

on the battery, 'twas beautiful to see it there in such a lovely spot. We saw the "big gun," & the sand works in Meeting St.—nothing, nothing but soldiers. The market was empty, not more than a dozen stalls had anything,—a calico dress costs $100.00 & a pair of shoes $66.00. We remained only a day as Tante was in a hurry.

No bombardment of the City while we were there, altho they fired a good deal at Sumter.

We went to see where the shells fell, they did not do much injury & so far *no one* in the City has been hurt by them.

Went to Augusta the other day and saw Beauregarde's sister and nieces, who are quite agreeable & informed us that Mr. John Barelli is *not* dead.

Aunt Ada & Uncle John ran the blockade from Wilmington in safety.

I have been sick a week. Doolie two weeks. Grandmother [DeCaradeuc] thinks of visiting Savannah & wishes me to go with her, I should like it *very* much.

Carrie [Griswold] has sent me some sweet, soothing lines composed on our boys, our dearest boys. Oh! can it be one year has gone & we have not seen them once, not heard from them, even now at mail time the same impatience comes over me that I always had for their sweet letters, and *forever* they are silent. Sometimes I wish I never had such a friend as Brother, one on whom my heart depended, & my life so linked, & then I never would have suffered so keenly in giving him up, but, then again, I would not have it otherwise, the remembrance of those days will ever be the oasis in my life. Mrs. McChesney's son, John Cochran,[11] is on our coast. We sent him a box & another is to go soon. I am to work a scarf and some more gloves for him, I sent him two pairs of gloves & some trifles of my own work, we cannot do enough for him. I am now knitting scarfs & gloves for a box Tante is getting up for the Marylanders who are cut off from their homes.

Dec. 6th, 1863

I hardly pretend to continue my journal regularly, I shall only write when I feel like it, home affairs & war affairs are so sad I haven't much heart for writing.

---

11. John H. Cochran was a private serving in the brigade of Brig. Gen. Henry A. Wise, engaged at this time in the coastal defenses of South Carolina.

Bragg has suffered a defeat—*no not a defeat*—but his handful of men after diabolical fighting & killing & wounding 40,000 Yankees, were overpowered by numbers & fell back to Chickamauga. Bragg has resigned. An officer of great intelligence from his army, says that his men love him & his enemies are only outside his army, that he has been censured much on account of not fighting Grant, but he was fully aware how 'twould be, that his army was too small to fight Grant's tremendous force.[12] Johnston has no army either & for the same reason Longstreet has to fall back on Virginia, rumor says Beauregarde must go out West. Gracious knows he is wanted there, he has fixed up Charleston harbor Yankee proof & a General less able can keep that point. The City is daily shelled, only two women have been killed & no fire has been, so far set by them, tho' many houses perforated. Money daily depreciates. Country people refuse now to receive the currency on the plea that they can get nothing for it, which is pretty nearly true, as a *cheap* calico or homespun dress costs $100.00 now, and one bushel corn $4.50 & $5.00, a pair turkey $35.00 & $40.00, nothing of the sort is now astonishing.

Dec. 29th, 1863

Well, since last I wrote here a good deal has happened, some of which I feel now like telling you, dear old Journal, so stop & listen.

Carrie Griswold came to see me a few days before Xmas and will stay with me the rest of the war, later her mother & aunt are to come too. Mother consenting to take them in for my sake, that I

---

12. The Battle of Chickamauga, Georgia, September 19–20, 1863, represented Gen. Braxton Bragg's greatest victory, albeit a pyrrhic one. Confederate losses were numbered at 2,312 dead, 14,674 wounded, and 1,468 missing. Federal losses were reported as 1,657 dead, 9,756 wounded, and 4,757 missing. Bragg's failure to follow up his tactical success was viewed by his critics as a wasted opportunity.

In the Battle of Missionary Ridge, November 25, 1863, Federal forces launched a frontal assault against the entrenched Confederates and drove them in disordered retreat back toward Chickamauga Creek south to Dalton, Georgia. Following this humiliating defeat Gen. Bragg requested relief from command. Bragg later commanded a division in the Army of Tennessee under Gen. Joseph E. Johnston. Faust, pp. 75, 133–37, 498–99; Hattaway and Jones, pp. 450–62.

may have my friends' companionship, they will provide for themselves & we will give them two rooms. Carrie, of course, Father says, will be my guest. The days before Xmas, we spent making gifts, and riding on horseback. On Christmas day we went to walk and met Father coming home with Mr. John H. Cochran, Mrs. McChesney's eldest son, he is on the coast with Wise's Brig. and Mother by dint of writing to his General, obtained a five day furlough to spend with us. He is quite handsome, nicely educated, and with very easy pleasant manner, and when he left this morning we all felt sorry to part, and all like him so much.

Cousin Maxine & Julia came over and stayed with us too, and we played all sorts of games, & had music, the first time I had touched the piano since the death of my darling Brothers. Oh! how strange it seemed to have a young man staying here who was not *their* guest & how I more than ever missed them.

Yesterday John Cochran & I walked together a very long walk, he made me tell him *all* about our boys & spoke *so* kindly to me. He says I am a magnet & draw him more closely to him every moment he spends with me, that he felt as tho he has known & loved me all his life, and wants me to correspond with him until he comes again, which, he says, will be, if he can get a furlough, in the spring. He told me of all his annoyances & troubles in camp, and I do feel the greatest interest in him. I made him a beautiful scarf, he said he valued it too highly to take it to Camp and sent it on to Virginia to his mother to keep for him. He says he never met with so congenial a mind as mine, and in truth we are alike. Mother continues to get beautiful letters from his mother; before he went this morning he told me so much about her. I think she must be an angel. He says I must know her one of these days; he told me again of his love, & I told him the same thing I did before, that I knew him too short a time for my heart to have been touched, but old Journal, there's that about him, which, I feel sure, time & acquaintance will put into my heart.

1864

Chapter Three

Wartime Travel:
Augusta on the Cars

Jan. 4th, 1864

I feel very sadly tonight, I cannot even speak of my own feelings to *anyone,* and because I always *think* them, with my little desk open on my knee & *sometime* write them here, because of this I think comes my devotion to my desk, 'twas Brother's too, he gave it to me to keep for him. Many & many is the thought coming from my inmost soul, which I have locked up here. I could never be lonely with my desk, my Bible & *my* copy of Tennyson.

We were summoned to my dear Grandmother [della Torre] this morning and were shocked by the change, the Dr. says there is no hope, & she cannot remain here long, the inevitable end, dreaded and battled against for two years, is now approaching, I dread to think of it, for us all, but most for Mother & Tante. Mother, as she is still bowed down in grief for her two noble boys, & such a blow so soon again for her, & Tante, poor Tante, her whole soul is in that aged Mother—; God grant us quiet, rest, & peace. Oh! 'tis too sad & sorrowful. Poor Mother! hardly has she understood her other trials before this great one has come to her.

Jan. 27th, 1864

Capt. Coxetter[1] and a Mr. somebody, I don't know how to spell his name, spent the morning here. The gentleman is a refu-

---

1. Capt. Louis M. Coxetter commanded the rebel privateer *Jeff Davis* in many successful raids on ships of the Union navy. As captain of the *Herald,* a steamer, he was equally successful in running the Federal blockade of Charleston. In February 1865 Coxetter's house near Aiken was burned, presumably by Brig.

gee from N. O. [New Orleans]. He is a young man, but his beard is quite white, he says he never had white hair until he lived under Beast Butler, and had to put up with the indignities & barbarities he inflicted. He says if two persons met on the street & commenced to talk, they were immediately joined by a U. S. soldier who either ordered them to disperse or listened to every word, if any opposition was offered they were taken to Ship Island in irons, man or woman, & if an officer should want a house, he looks about for one to suit him, goes over it, & if all is as he wished, tells the owner and his family, he has need of his house and furniture, to leave by the next morning eight o'clock, if any one should say even "what a shame" he is put in irons & sent to Ship Island, as being guilty of dangerous words.

The *ladies* whom circumstances unhappily compelled to take the oath of allegience to Lincoln, had to sign it before a *Negro man*, one lady's hand trembled whilst she was writing, and the impudent demon—perhaps fresh from a cotton plantation,— had the audacity to take her hand & hold it down, talking most insolently & *abominally* the while. One gentleman wanted some paper for leaving the City, & went to the Beast for it, he was referred to *"Major Green,"* in some other street, upon asking for him, "Major Green" proved to be his own coachman, a horrid black negro, hand in glove with the Beast. Oh! I cannot tell all. The refugees were allowed to depart with ten days' rations & the clothes on their backs, nothing more, silver, clothing, jewels, *everything* else had to be left to the Beast and his vile associates.[2]

Gen. Hugh Judson Kilpatrick's Federal forces foraging and raiding in the area at this time. *ORN*, I, 17, pp. 213–14; SHC: Cornish Diary, Feb. 22, 1865. For a detailed account of Confederate blockade running during the Civil War see: Stephen R. Wise, *Lifeline of the Confederacy, Blockade Running During the Civil War* (1988).

2. On May 1, 1862, Maj. Gen. Benjamin F. Butler occupied the city of New Orleans and imposed stringent martial law. He immediately instituted a number of controversial and unpopular orders designed to quell the rebellious citizenry and restore law and order. The most controversial order and, perhaps, the one which most contributed to the sobriquet "Beast Butler" was the so-called woman order issued May 15, 1862: ". . . it is ordered that hereafter when any female shall by word, gesture or movement, insult or show contempt for any officer or soldier of the United States, she shall be regarded and held liable to be treated as a woman of the town plying her avocation." James Parton, *General Butler in New Orleans, History of the Administration of the Department of the Gulf in the Year 1862*, 1864, pp. 279–354; OR, I, 6, pp. 715–25.

He told us many more instances of horror & degradation. My blood almost boiled as I listened. Capt. Coxetter in his turn gave us some good accounts of his escapes & daring adventure on water with the privateer. And a full detail of the Trent affair long ago and how Miss Slidell slapped the Yankee Fairfax's face in defending her father. We were much interested.[3]

I never mentioned that Miss Hessie and Mrs. Griswold are with us, as refugees for the war, of course, my Carrie too, they have been here nearly a month.

Mr. & Mrs. Walker & Meta Heyward[4] spent this morning with us. Meta has just returned from Savannah, and her account increases our desire to visit it, we go in the spring, if nothing prevents.

The Yankees still shell the City, the houses are perforated & every one has moved up town out of reach of them, every thing like business there is in complete confusion. Every thing now is distressing, poor Mr. Henry is deranged, nothing but the state of affairs has caused it, I know.

Jan. 30th, 1864

I do not often feel like writing here now, there are events enough to record if I choose, people come & go, but I don't care for them, I feel, well it's of no use to say how I do feel. I subscribed to "*Personne's*" paper hoping to find entertainment there, but am somewhat disappointed. I send them in Mother's name to John Cochran on the coast.

Conversation this evening introduced Major S., consequently led me into a few backward thoughts of what an infatuated crea-

3. On November 8, 1861, the Union warship *San Jacinto* fired two shots across the bow of the British mail packet *Trent*, 240 miles from Cuba, bound for the British West Indies. A boarding party under the command of executive officer Lt. D. M. Fairfax arrested and forcibly removed two Confederate commissioners, James M. Mason and John Slidell, and their secretaries, George Eustis and J. E. MacFarland. The four men were then transported to Ft. Warren in Boston Harbor. The incident almost brought the Union to the brink of war with Great Britain. For a full account of the incident see *ORN*, I, 1, pp. 129–202.
4. Margaret Heyward (Meta), age 22, resided in Aiken with her parents, Mr. and Mrs. Jonathan Thomas Heyward. Mr. and Mrs. William Walker lived near Aiken.

ture he was, how I disliked, all but dispised him, and showed him so plainly, and yet—and—yet—well I feel sadly amused when I think what followed the evening he left for the war. Ah! me. I'm getting sleepy now.

Mrs. G.[riswold] heard that my dear old friend Mr. Henry is hopelessly insane, I am too sad about it, trust 'tisn't true, poor dear old gentleman; he was so uniformly kind to me.

The girls want to go over to Augusta on Saturday, I'll go along too to hear of him, and to try to get poor Western Thomas' picture.[5] I think his aunt will give it, and I'm most anxious to have one.

Feb. 14th, 1864

Carrie and I went over to Augusta yesterday, and really in spite of everything had a very amusing time. We bought several photographs of our most illustrious Gen's. I got Lee, Davis & Kirby Smith. John Cochran sent me word the other day that he had sent out to Richmond for Stonewall Jackson's for me, so that I'll have that too.

We visited Mr. Henry who is better, also Mrs. Foster, Mrs. Tubman & Mother's old friend, Mrs. Campbell. Then we tried to shop, but the only thing in the shape of a dress for myself that we saw, was a worsted stuff at $30.00 a yard.

I met Lieut. Col. Croft[6] who stopped me & talked awhile on the street, he is most dreadfully, *agonizingly*, wounded in his right hand & looks very badly.

When we finished our business we sauntered round to the church yard & sat there 'till time to meet the train. When we reached the depot there was such a concourse of soldiers there that I begged an old lady who was going too, to let us remain with her. I was very uneasy as I never was in a crowd of men without a

---

5. Probably a reference to Brig. Gen. Edward Lloyd Thomas, CSA, a wealthy Georgia planter.
6. Lt. Col. Edward Croft of the 14th Regiment of the South Carolina Infantry [McGowan's Brigade] sustained wounds at the Battle of Cold Harbor in 1862; at Gettysburg in 1863; and later at Hatcher's Run [Petersburg] in 1865. Caldwell, *The History of a Brigade of South Carolinians* .... 1866; rpt., 1951, pp. 70, 213.

protector before, however, a young & handsome soldier came up & introduced himself, Major Beaufort[7] of Va. and begged us to allow him to remain near us until the car was opened. When the doors were unlocked we got in & obtained good seats, some twenty-five ladies had to stand up & as many had to be left, & such crowds of soldiers!! An officer in front of us spread his blanket on the seat & begged us to keep it for him, but 'twas impossible & he couldn't even get in the car again. After a little while I heard a plaintive voice outside under the window, say: "Oh, Miss Pauline, ain't there any room in there for me?" I looked out & saw Col. Croft, of course, he couldn't get in our car; he asked me to look for his cousin in our car who was wounded & on crutches, but I couldn't even move, after talking a while he went into the con-ductor's car then I heard another voice say: "Miss Pauline, can't you get me a seat in front of you? I want to get in your car so much." What could I do? He was a very handsome Capt. I felt assured I knew him, his face & voice were perfectly familiar, but I could not remember his name, he conversed for awhile just like some old friend, seemed to know me well, but I don't yet remem-ber who he is. Anyhow *he* too had to go off. Then our Va. Major came under the window to chat, & I gave him some cake I bought for the children, they would not allow soldiers to come in our car, without a lady; meanwhile a soldier on crutches stood near us looking sick & weak, he *stood* of course, & Carrie, noble as she always is rose & insisted on his taking her seat, but he would not hear of it, he then introduced himself, Captain Croft, the cousin, the Lieut. Col. asked me to look for, he remained with us the rest of the time & proved to be most agreeable.

After awhile we looked up & there was our kind Virginia Major standing by us, he pretended to the conductor that he had to see us out, & thus got into our car from which he did not again move, he is really quite charming & entertained us very nicely, two more Captains spoke to us & offered to assist us in any way, but our Va. friend didn't give them a chance, he saw us to the carriage at Johnston's & all but cried when we got off the car. I think somehow we will hear of him again, he was 'mazin kind & attentive to us, should like to return it.

---

7. Major T. A. Buford, 34th Regiment, Virginia Volunteers.

March 16th, 1864

The sum total of events at home for the past few days is, that we have walked a good deal, been on the cars, those adventurous cars, to Aiken & back, took a seven miles' ride with that "hard case" Jimmie McDonald, found cantering by far the most interesting item of it. Finished plaiting and making . . . [illegible]

. . . [illegible] they are such unprincipled outlaws, this morning they brought a band of their friends along with them who remained secreted in the woods in case of need. I heartily wish them all in the army—the miserable conscripts.

The gentlemen are going to have them arrested, besides having them prosecuted for resisting the law & stealing the stills seized by Government. I don't know how all this will end.

All the talk is about the unfortunate currency, and thousands and one taxes, tho few, very few complain. Butter is $10.00 a pound in Augusta. Flour $200.00 per barrel. Currency, currency, nothing but that. $50.00 to have one tooth filled.

March 26th, 1864

We had snow on the 22nd. Fa. pelted us girls, that is, Carrie, Mannie,[8] cousin Maxine & myself famously & we gave it back to him, with interest.

All the fruit is killed.

For Government purposes the night train has stopped, and persons, except soldiers can only travel on business. Poor Dr. Bruns has lost his sweet wife.

A gentleman from Charleston, Sanders by name, spent the night here.

March 31st, 1864

I took a long ride on horseback, with my dearest Father, away down on the runs, to Mrs. Glovers, how I love to be with him & how many of those delightful rides he has taken me,—dear Fa.

---

8. Mannie was Margaret Ann DeCaradeuc, Pauline's younger sister, born in 1849 at Montmorenci.

Mrs. Hankinson met me & oh! how she spoke of our peerless boys, her sons are in the Company in which they [Frank and Tonio] were,[9] she says that they were the best of the Company, that as to Antonio, everybody loved him & her boys told her that he didn't know how to do any real wrong, that the men all loved him, for his goodness, his sunny heart, his pure almost guilness conversation & even old men respected him for his daring courage. Ah! how that powerful, quiet innate courage impressed all who were near him, even when he was a little child. When only thirteen years of age at school, the grown boys of sixteen to nineteen used to respect him so, & his precocious bravery made him so much their equal that they were his companions, how often & often have I seen him then, arm & arm with a boy of six or seven years his senior, a boy with a moustache, who would consider it derogatory to associate with younger boys, but to Tonio, they were companions, and many of them used to come home with him in the holidays, he impressed all and yet he was a child, an innocent pure child to the last. At school and in his company he was the favorite & at both, they called him their "first & foremost." Young Bull who saw him only one or two times in Aiken, came here not long ago to beg to be allowed to visit his grave, he was quite a stranger but admired Tonio so much. Mrs. H. said that the men all *loved* Tonio so much & looked up to Brother, whenever any speech, or writing was to be made or done, they all wished him, & when calm, cool, resource & perfect intrepedity was quoted he was always the one brought up. All this & so much more we know, but I cannot hear enough of them. I wished so much to ask more of them, but the mere accidental mention of either name completely upsets me, and I did not dare trust my voice before a stranger.

The other day I received a letter addressed to Miss Pauline Colorado, & found it to be from the Virginia Major we met on the car, T. A. Buford by name, quite a handsome note begging me to accept an accompanying piece of music, as a slight testimonial of his high appreciation of my sentiments towards Va., and of my kind offers to himself; I believe I told him something or other about if he ever required the services of a friend in S. C. he would

---

9. Probably a reference to the family of Milledge and Sarah Hankinson, landholders in the area, among whose children were John, age 24, and Alfred, age 18.

find a ready one in my Father who considered it a privilege to do anything for the Virginians, I said something of the sort when he shook hands at the carriage that night, then I came home and was quietly forgetting him. I wrote him a note of acknowledgement this morning.

Chapter Four

Sojourn in Savannah:
A Respite from the War

April 4th, 1864

Grandmother has appointed the 8th for our departure for Savannah, Fannie Morell will not be there, so I do not anticipate a very agreeable time, 'tis indifferent to me now, however, although I have a great wish to visit the place.

Mother received one of Mrs. McChesney's beautiful letters, she always mentions my own dearest Brother so beautifully, I love to read her letters, one of my dearest wishes is to know her, *she* is, if ever there was one, a *perfect* woman, her son is still on our coast, and expects soon to go home to Va. I wish for his mother's sake, he would come again to see us before he goes. I really cannot understand myself, it seems to me I am all different, and my strongest feeling is one of continual longing, & for what? I cannot know, the effect is powerful in my heart, but the cause, I cannot discover. It makes me quite miserable sometimes, I trust it won't last much longer,—eh bien, mon ami, what next?

April 6th, 1864

Mr. Sanders came from town and will spend the week with us, he has bought our mill and is seeing about it, not clever, but agreeable, a Mr. Cross also, came from the City, on business to Fa. & spent the day & night here, and today Mr. Peay spent with us, he is a young & pleasant soldier, brother to the one about whom they used to tease me at the camp, when he went & sent me a newspaper, one which I wished, & sent word he was coming soon again to see me, much obliged to him, but hope to be soon in Savannah.

Carrie and I dined at [Rose Hill] yesterday, we went & returned on horseback.

This afternoon I spent in our precious little cemetery, near my own darling Brothers, the flowers there are superlatively lovely.

Savannah, April 11th, 1864

We left home on the 8th and reached this City on the 9th. We are staying with Grandmother's niece & my cousin, Mrs. Macdonald, they are strangers to me, but so far, I am very much pleased with both Mr. and Mrs. Macdonald,[1] they seem to be so genuinely good & true hearted. Cousin Mack [Mrs. MacDonald] took us to church yesterday, where I heard, what I have been longing to hear for a long while, some real sweet church music, one voice there is very fine. Carrie came to see me yesterday, too, & Mr. and Mrs. O'Driscol[2] called on us after church. In the afternoon we walked in the Park[3] which is one of the most beautiful places I have ever visited. Clara Gregg is married to Nat Chafee— wish her joy with him.

I went to see Mrs. Prendergast this afternoon, her son[4] was intimate with Brother, & Brother did everything for him in his last moments & had his grave railed in & fixed so sweetly. I felt much on seeing her & she seemed the same. She begged me to give her a likeness of Brother, I saw one of Farley which she had. I hear Mary Farley[5] is here, how I should like to see her.

---

1. Mr. and Mrs. Donald MacDonald lived in Savannah on the S.E. corner of Lincoln and Gaston Streets. Mr. MacDonald was treasurer of the Albany & Gulf Railroad.
2. W. C. O'Driscoll was a Savannah merchant. The O'Driscolls lived on Liberty Street.
3. Forsyth Park was named in 1851 for John Forsyth, former governor, who also served as Secretary of State under Presidents Andrew Jackson and Martin Van Buren. It was a beautifully landscaped park which by 1858 boasted an attractive fountain believed to be the largest in the country at that time. Sieg, *The Squares, An Introduction to Savannah*, 1984, p. 224.
4. J. J. Prendergast was listed as killed in action on the Roll of Honor of soldiers from Savannah serving in the Civil War.
5. Mary Farley, age 20, was the daughter of W. R. Farley, a lawyer of Laurensville. Her brother, Lt. W. D. Farley, who died at Gettysburg, was a friend of Pauline's brother Frank.

April 12th, 1864

After breakfast Cousin Mack took us to visit the stores, we had a pleasant walk, and had a much better view of the City, 'tis the most beautiful one I have ever been in, and I receive so much kindness from my cousins, the most delicate kindness.

In the afternoon, a Capt. Barnwell called for me to go to walk, he is quite agreeable, he told me that a Capt. in his Regt. told him he had seen my picture, & that, if I looked like it, I must be very beautiful. Another Captain, Maxwell by name, saw it too, and begged Capt. B. to bring him to see me.[6] While we were walking around the Park, a very pretty girl came up & introduced herself to me as Miss Farley, how rejoiced I was to see her, & I mean to call on her tomorrow. Capt. Barnwell escorted Cousin Mack & me to the theater, where the best amateurs gave a delightful concert, I enjoyed it very much, the hall was greatly crowded, but we had a most pleasant time.

April 13th, 1864

I went to see Mary Farley, she is extremely pretty & intelligent with great animation of manner. I sat some time with her & know I'll like her—I felt much on seeing her.

In the afternoon several visitors called, Mrs. & Miss Prendergast among others, the former brought me a beautiful picture of Farley [W.D.] to look at, how *very* handsome he was, & how I love his memory, I have always thought him to be my fate, this his sister told me they used to think.

Carrie came to see me from the Cohens, where she is staying, authorized by Miss Cohen to invite me there to go with them to a church wedding and from there to spend the night at their house, I went and enjoyed Carrie's society much.

---

6. Capt. A. Smith Barnwell commanded Barnwell's Georgia Battery in the District of Georgia under Brig. Gen. Hugh W. Mercer. Capt. J. A. Maxwell commanded Maxwell's Battery (A), Georgia Artillery, in the District of Georgia under Brig. Gen. Mercer. *OR*, I, 35, pt. 2, p. 458.

April 14th, 1864

Carrie came back & spent the day here with me, Mary Farley called, and spent a part of the morning with me, and Mrs. & Frank O'Driscol paid us a visit.

April 18th, 1864

It has been raining very much, I went to church three times yesterday, they have delightful music there, one voice is very superior. Mary Farley went with me in the morning, after vespers we walked in the thronged Park.

April 20th, 1864

I went after breakfast to walk with Cousin Mack & Grand-mother, stopped at the dress makers to have a military jacket cut out for myself, on my return I had a visit from Onie Legriel & Marie LaCoste.

After dinner Mr. MacDonald took us in a steamer to visit the obstructions & fortifications on the river, I was very much inter-ested in Fort Jackson.[7]

Mary Farley and Carrie called here in the afternoon.

April 24th, 1864

Yesterday Capt. Barnwell and Lieut. Richardson[8] dined here. Capt. Barnwell took me to walk, he is devoted & marked in his attentions to me, and in every way remarkably kind, he returned here to tea and I played on the piano 'till near ten o'clock. I enjoyed yesterday very much.

---

7. Fort Jackson was a masonry fort a few miles east of Savannah guarding the south channel of the Savannah River.
8. Lt. W. S. Richardson was an artillery officer stationed at Fort Pemberton, James Island, South Carolina. *OR*, I, 35, pt. 2, p. 509.

Home, May 12th, 1864

We returned on the 10th after spending a month in Savannah; if I had been in another frame of mind, I should have enjoyed it very, very much, but this unaccountable something buried in my heart worries me so, nobody knows it though, for my,—external— spirits are better than they have been for a year, and all think Savannah has been of great service to me. If kind and plentiful attention, & admiration could have influenced me, I should have been better, for I received a great deal of it in Savannah, but *that* is *not* what I want, it don't satisfy me. I am unreasonable & wicked I know, I cannot pray altho, sometimes I'm over an hour on my knees trying to turn to God as I used to, persons think me more devout, but it's like my spirits, empty.

Chapter Five

A Heavy Heart:
Losses in the Virginia Campaigns

May 23, 1864

I have no heart to keep this Journal or tell of the dreadful,
fatal battles in Va. Oh my God! my heart is too heavy, I am
entirely miserable. Many whom I know are killed & wounded.
Robert Taft and Col. Shooter are killed. Capt. Barnwell killed.
George Lalane wounded.[1] Wise's Brigade was subjected to a fearful firing from the enemy at Druery's Bluff.[2] I suppose John
Cochran is wounded, from the moment I saw him I felt that his
life would be given to this devouring war; and I am assured that
he is dead or wounded, for I *feel it.* [The following was added
later:] That day two months after, he was killed in Va. I believe
my heart is frozen.

May 31st, 1864

I have nothing to write, but feel like it. I have been sick in
bed two days, & am just out of it, Carrie & I are studying French

---

1. Lt. Robert M. Taft, 25th South Carolina Volunteers, died May 17, 1864, of
wounds received the day before while storming the enemy lines at Drewry's
Bluff. Lt. Col. Washington P. Shooter, commanding the First Regiment, South
Carolina Volunteers (McGowan's Brigade), was shot and killed at Spottsylvania, May 12, 1864. Capt. John Gibbes Barnwell, Company H, First South
Carolina Volunteers (McGowan's Brigade), was reported wounded, not killed,
in the Battle of the Wilderness, May 5–7, 1864. He recovered from his wounds
and is later reported on the muster roll of August 31, 1864 as "absent wounded,"
having sustained wounds in July 1864 near Petersburg. Lt. George M. Lalane
subsequently died of his wounds. *Richmond Enquirer,* May 13, 1864; *OR,* I,
28, pt. 1, p. 485; Salley, I, pp. 215, 329–30; Caldwell, pp. 136, 146, 149, 174.
2. Brig. Gen. Henry A. Wise, CSA, reported 18 killed and 75 wounded, May
16–20, 1864, in his brigade's defense of Drewry's Bluff on the James River, 5
miles below Richmond. *OR,* I, 36, pt. 2, p. 261.

diligently, I practice hard, read Shakespeare, & history every day, I still devote from nine to one o'clock to St. Julien & Frank Coffin,[3] it's over a year now since I have been so doing, this occupies my mind in a measure.

Mary Farley has written to ask me to commence a correspondence in French, with her. I will do so. Her brother Hugh is badly wounded.[4] At home here, we have much sickness, Tante has been ill in my room for nearly two months with spinal disease; for the same length of time Miss Hessie has been confined to her room suffering from a dreadful fall. All the children have had varioloide,[5] & now mumps are going the rounds. Mrs. Griswold & Carrie are sick with neuralgia.

I never mentioned here that I received a piece of music accompanied by a courteous note from Major T. A. Buford of 34th Va. Regt. Vol. I accepted it & acknowledged its receipt by a note, he *respectfully opened a correspondence* which in consideration of his courtesy & kindness on the cars, and of his being an entire stranger in our State, I joined. His credentials from John C. being first rate; he is now in Va., has been in all the battles recently fought in the Wilderness, & Oh God! if there Thou has called him, pardon his offences & receive his soul.

Gen. McGowan,[6] my kind friend, is severely wounded, Capt. Brooks,[7] Brother's intimate & valued friend, is dangerously wounded.

---

3. St. Julien DeCaradeuc, Pauline's younger brother, was born in 1854 at Montmorenci. Frank Coffin was the son of Dr. and Mrs. Amory Coffin of Aiken.
4. Hugh L. Farley, Co. G, Third Regiment, South Carolina Volunteers, had served as aide-de-camp to Gen. Joseph B. Kershaw in the Battle of Chickamauga and was highly commended for his gallantry. Apparently he was wounded in the Virginia campaigns of 1864. *OR*, I, 30, pt. 2, p. 506; Salley, 2, pp. 465–66.
5. Varioloid usually referred to a mild form of smallpox occurring in those partially protected by previous vaccination. In all likelihood Pauline was referring to chicken pox.
6. Brig. Gen. Samuel McGowan of Abbeville, South Carolina, received a severe wound on May 12, 1864, at Spottsylvania Court House, in the battle of "bloody angle." He survived the war and was elected Associate Justice of the State Supreme Court in 1879. *CMH*, 5, pp. 318, 412–14; Brooks, *South Carolina Bench and Bar*, 1908, p. 75.
7. Capt. John H. Brooks, Seventh South Carolina Battalion, received three severe wounds at Drewry's Bluff, May 16, 1864. He was commended for gallantry by Brig. Gen. Johnson Hagood. *OR*, I, 36, pt. 2, pp. 253–54; *CMH*, 5, p. 322.

May 31st, 1864

Cols. Aldrich & Walker spent yesterday & last night with us,[8] & left this morning. I have promised to pay a visit to Miss Aldrich this summer. I am so glad that I am at last successfully able to command my strong feelings. Yesterday news came that George Lalane, poor, dear George, is mortally wounded, no one knew of the pain, keen pain I felt, as the blood seemed to rush from my heart, for some time I did not dare to speak, but when I did, I was astonished at myself to see how I could hide what I felt, in spite of self-reproach & sorrow for apparent unkindness. I never really loved him, though at one time I thought I did, but if any one ever loved me truly & devotedly, it was he, I have always felt the strongest interest & friendship for him, my poor friend! My God, pity him, spare him. On account of Mother & Father's great dislike & objection to anything serious between us, his name has been rarely uttered at home, and knowing why, I have never openly showed how much I like him, *poor* fellow, and now no one need know how I sorrow for him. Tante suspected tho', I think, for after hearing it yesterday, I went to hand her something and my hand touched hers, she started at their icyness & looked me earnestly in the face, after a while, she put her arms 'round me & kissed me, calling me "poor baby." I could have cried with all my heart, but thank gracious, I did not, but I *smiled*, kissed her as usual, and went down stairs with the family. Ah me! just to think of all our dying & wounded in Va. and the last order from the War department, prevents *anyone* from going there, whether for sick relatives or anything else. Oh God! of mercy end this desolating cruelty.

---

8. Col. Alfred Proctor Aldrich of Barnwell, South Carolina, served on the staffs of Gen. M. L. Bonham and Gen. Maxcy Gregg. He remained in active service until after the battle of Manassas when he suffered an injury in a railroad accident which disabled him. He became a circuit judge in 1865. Col. Joseph Walker of Spartanburg commanded the regiment of Palmetto Sharpshooters in Brig. Gen. Micah Jenkins' Brigade, Maj. Gen. Charles W. Fields' Division of the First Army Corps under the command of Lt. Gen. James Longstreet. Brooks, p. 153; *OR*, I, 36, pt. 1, p. 1022; Garlington, *Men of the Time* . . . , 1902, pp. 429–30.

June 2nd, 1864

This day brought tidings of George Lalane's death. Oh how much sorrow is in my heart this night. I did not love him as he loved me, but I have watched his rising steps thro this war with a fond, tender interest, and I have lost one very dear to me. Ah! poor, poor fellow, to have died so young, with so many bright hopes! and with such a complete and sad misunderstanding with me. Such a noble future his brave deeds were winning for him.

I went down stairs for the mail, Cousin Maxine handed me the paper, & with the eagerness, common to some people, to impart bad news, said, "Young Lalane is dead, died in Va. hospital." I hoped *so much*, that it shocked me fearfully, I felt cold all over, but I took the paper, read the editorial on him myself, then went to my Brother's grave, where I let all my feelings have vent.

While kneeling there, a fearful storm of wind & rain arose, it accorded with my feelings, and I stayed there.

When I came into my room to remove my wet clothing, Mother came in, put her arms 'round me & we wept together.

I have a letter from him just before the first bloody battle of this war, in speaking of it—(he was then marching to the field of action)—he said, then, "For my countrie and my lady love, & if I die unloved, I hope it will not be unhonored or unloved." Neither unhonored, unwept or unloved, dear, dear George, now that you have solved that drear enigma—death. Long, long, will your sweet name move my heart, and ascend on my unworthy prayers of supplicating mercy to our God,—Oh, I am too dreary and sorrowful this night.

June 18th, 1864

I have not felt like writing all these days, every one has been commenting on my looks, and nearly all of the family think me sick.

Grandmother & Mother tell me I'm pale 'till I'm green, but I am not sick, and I can't bear them to notice me.

Carrie went over to Augusta soon after the 2nd of June & stayed four days, so that I enjoyed the luxury of a room by myself, when I most wished it. There is nothing more soothing or charming to me than my own room, only let it be *my own* & I care not where or what it is. I have been a *long* time without it now, & often wish things were as they used to be, of late my room (or rather Mannie's, for I have given up mine to Tante for seven weeks) well, Mannie's room has been stretched to three & four at a time.

Our family is some days numbered at sixteen, thirteen being now the usual number and I feel so like quiet, and *only home around*; it's unamiable to feel so, but tho I never show it, I feel it. I write a heap here of what no one could dream I ever felt.

My inner life is entirely & essentially different from my outer. My heart most usually bleeds inwardly, and this Journal is the only thing in this world that ever gets a peep into it, it's a comfort for me to write here sometimes; my desk is *so* private, so entirely my own.

Lizzie Coffin[9] came down & spent four or five days with me. The Yankees on the coast are preparing for a raid through our state to Augusta, the Garrison at the arsenal there have been officially notified to be on the alert to receive them, the raiders would pass within a mile & a half of us, and as they carry the torch & rapine with them always, most people are very uneasy, I assisted Fa. in trimming bullets, &c. and we have two rifles & three pistols ready loaded in case they should come this way.

All here think that in the event of their coming I would be quite cool, I think & hope I would be, should *not* like the ordeal by any means.

The outer works at Petersburg, Va. have been carried by the enemy, only desperate skill & fighting can save it & keep Richmond from being a steadily Beleagued City. Only two Brigades are there (Petersburg) Wise's and another.[10] A letter came from

---

9. Eliza Coffin, age 19, was the daughter of Dr. and Mrs. Amory Coffin of Aiken.
10. The garrison defending Petersburg against the attack on June 9, 1864, by Brig. Gen. August V. Kautz's U. S. cavalry division consisted only of Wise's infantry brigade numbering 2,400; Sturdivant's light battery of 4 guns; about 25 guns in the main redans; and some 300 citizens (a militia of old men and boys). These citizen soldiers led by Brig. Gen. Raleigh E. Colston and Maj. F. H. Archer fought against overwhelming numbers and repulsed two frontal cavalry attacks. The time bought by their heroism temporarily saved their city. *OR*, I, pt. 2, 36, pp. 310–19. Also see Gary W. Gallagher, ed., *Fighting for the Confederacy, The Personal Recollections of General Edward Porter Alexander* (1989), pp. 419–34.

John Cochran, dated from the rifle pits of Petersburg, their brigade has suffered severely, so far he is safe, tho' has had some
narrow escapes.

I think the crisis of the whole war is at hand, the Yankees
must do *all* they can before the approaching Presidential election,
& they haven't much time left them.

Yesterday morning, Jabe alarmed us all by falling down suddenly in a dreadful fit in the pantry. In the afternoon, Mother had
an alarming nervous chill, and at night Tante was very sick.
Grandmother, too, was sick in bed, & several of the servants,
didn't I have my hands full?

July 17th, 1864

I returned yesterday from the Sand Hills near Augusta,[11]
where I have been spending a week with the Redmonds,[12] I enjoyed
it exceedingly, every day we went to the Arsenal to make cartridges under the supervision of Col. Reins, I like it very much
and made 3,200 in three days, this was very slow compared to
what the others did. The Government is pressed for them and the
ladies are called upon to meet its requisitions. The ladies on the
hill turn out 30,000 a day, those in the city of Augusta do equally
as well.[13]

While on the Hill I met Capt. John Milledge,[14] with whom I
was very much pleased, he was quite devoted to me, said lots of
fine and sweet things, and—ended by getting me to promise to
correspond with him, he is a splended musician and really his
attentions were quite charming.

11. Sandhills Village was located in the upcountry of Richmond County, 3 miles
west of Augusta. Originally designed as a summer resort for low country
planters, the community was located on a high sandy hill where the water
was pure and the climate deemed healthy.
12. The Redmond family were living in Berzelia, Georgia, in Columbia County,
20 miles west of Augusta.
13. The Augusta Arsenal, one of five Confederate arsenals, had been seized from
the Federal forces on January 24, 1861, just 5 days after Georgia's secession
from the Union. Under the supervision of Maj. Josiah Gorgas the Augusta
Arsenal was producing 20,000 to 30,000 rounds of rifle cartridges and 125 to
150 rounds of field ammunition on a daily basis. Faust, p. 30.
14. Capt. John Milledge, Jr., Artillery, Georgia Battery, Nelson's Brigade.

I had a real fine week. On the way home I met Col. McCreary[15] who sat by me, fanning me, 'till I reached Johnstons. I was glad to meet him because he told me so much about my friends in Va.

Oh dear me! what an enigma I had solved for me, by Nellie Redmond, here it is, lying on her bed, she asked me if I had ever been in love, I told her never really; she expressed great surprise, so much indeed, that I asked her what she meant, she said that the family believed that I was at one time very much attached to Amo Coffin,[16] that Lizzie told her, they all thought I cared for Amo, that he loved me, they knew, and that the great difference of faith was all that kept it from "being a match," he is so devoted to his religion & I to mine, that it would not do, consequently he has done all in his power to keep from me, out of danger, & is hard at work forgetting me now.

This is just exactly the motive I attached to the sudden cessation of his attention to me, when I used to see him so often—mais —he needn't be afraid, for I am sure nothing cd. ever have induced me to *lose my heart with him (out of the army & only 23 years)*, though *long, long* ago, I believe, I did like him a great deal, but I hadn't any sense then, now that I think of it, I really believe, Mrs. C. has been feeling very sorry for me all this time, all that she has told me about him &c. what a pity that so much of her surplus sympathy should have been wasted, & really I never have seen any of them without asking about Amo, & have patiently listened to many of his letters, &c. from little interest in him, & to flatter the vanity of his too proud Mama, unconscious that 'twas done in commiseration of me—so be it—what next?

July 26th, 1864

Estelle Allison[17] came down and spent five days with us, she is such a lively, bright, pleasant girl that I was really sorry to

15. Col. C. W. McCreary, First South Carolina Regiment (Infantry, Provisional Army), McGowan's Brigade, had sustained wounds at Spottsylvania May 12, 1864. *OR*, I, 36, pt. 2, p. 792.
16. Amory Coffin, Jr., son of Dr. and Mrs. Amory Coffin of Aiken, was a graduate of the South Carolina Military Academy (The Citadel). In December of 1864 he sustained a head wound in a skirmish near Cosawhatchie, South Carolina. The Coffins were communicants of St. Thaddeus' Episcopal Church in Aiken. Cornish Papers 1461, SHC: December 8, 1864, Diary entry.
17. Estelle Allison, age 19, was the daughter of S. L. Allison, a railroad agent,

give her up, we rode and amused ourselves very agreeably, during her visit.

Today a long letter from John Cochran came, he is well, he has been in every engagement around Petersburg.

August 3rd, 1864

Cordes Boylston has a son, how funny, he's nothing but a boy himself nor will he ever be anything else.

Mrs. Gibbes & Phoebe[18] dined with us today, & as usual had a plenty of pleasant chat, and sang us some pretty new songs. Dear Robbie, is very sick, on the coast. From his association with my noble Tonio, he *is* too dear to me, & I pray God may spare him to his widowed mother.

Carrie & I had a magnificent ride a cheval, this afternoon, and after supper, we read some real funny things together.

August 4th, 1864

After breakfast this morning, while practicing, Mother sent for me, I found her in the pantry, weeping bitterly over a notice of John Cochran's death.[19] What a frightful shock this was to me, and how sudden is death! he was killed at Petersburg on the 21st July. Poor, poor fellow, many bitter tears, have I this day shed over his untimely end, tears for him, for I felt an attachment for him, good & noble as he must have been, as I *know* he was, & tears of love & sympathy for his poor Mother who was so, so much to my precious Brother on his deathbed, how my heart aches for her, if I could only put my arms around her neck & weep with her, & tell her how I honored that son who was so much to her. We all feel as tho death has carried from us one of our own, for he was so

living in Aiken. She later became the second wife of Lt. Col. Theodore Gaillard Croft, M. D. *Confederate Veteran*, 23, 1, Jan. 1915, p. 366.

18. Mrs. Gibbes and Phoebe, age 15, lived in nearby Graniteville, in Edgefield County. Robert M. (Robbie), age 19, was serving in the Confederate army at this time.

19. Pvt. John H. Cochran, age 24, was killed in the trenches near Petersburg, Va., on July 21, 1864. *Richmond Enquirer*, August 9, 1864.

sociable and pleasantly at home with us here, and *so hopeful*, poor fellow & so confident. I don't know how to write what I feel for him. My heart is so full, I feel all the time like reproaching myself too, for what, I do not know, for he himself told me, when I begged him not to think me unkind, that he could not think so when he approved of my course himself, poor fellow, he had no time to prove himself, as he said, save to crown a perfect life with a glorious death.

Chapter Six

Travel and Trepidation: A Visit to Columbia, Sherman's Troops Threaten

August 17th, 1864

Our quiet routine has been broken into of late.
As far as I remember, I will write in what way. I have felt, *oh so sadly* though all the time for my poor friend's death.
On Monday, Carrie asked me to go to Aiken with her. Saw Amo, Oh, dear! for the first time in many months, he didn't try to avoid me, but seemed delighted. I wasn't, anyway.
In the afternoon, while asleep in our room, Mother brought me a note from Nellie Redmond saying, she, Mel, & Capt. Jack Milledge were at the R.R. waiting to be sent for.
They wrote to say they were coming, but we didn't get their letter. We sent for them & they came. Capt. Jack went on to Va. after we met in Augusta, stayed three weeks, & told me that *black eyes* lured him back. One thing, (en passant) *black eyes sent him off* for good, this time.
The man seemed perfectly infatuated, he seemed so in Augusta & tho, Nellie told me she knew he was seriously taken, I thought it a flirtation on both sides, and was astounded to hear of his return & to see him. I like him, but some of his attributes are hideous to my mind,—over fond of *agua vitia*, he only stayed one day & night, & then carried his walking ticket *back to Va.* That man will marry for money, I know. He played & sang some beautiful music for me, this he does *beautifully*. Well, Capt. Jack, enough of *you* now.
I sent for Lizzie, Amo & Anna Lesesne to come down & stay with us while the Redmonds would be here, the girls came and being seven of us, we had every kind of fun and frolic imaginable. Mel is very smart & amusing, she & John Milledge are intimate, she is crazy for me to tell her if I 'brought him to terms,' as she

strongly suspects, but as *he* hasn't told her, I certainly shant, and I won't tell any of these girls, what's the use?

They all spent the week with me and I believe we all enjoyed ourselves splendidly, altho we had no beaux.

I hope to go to Columbia soon, am crazy to get there. I enjoyed Nellie's music so much, she sings very prettily, she, Mel & Capt. John M. sang us some delightful songs, on the table rock in the moonlight, he has a remarkably rich voice.

Torriani is to teach in Augusta, Nellie wants me to go over & take lessons from him with her. Wish I only could.

August 24th, 1864

Mary Gregg & Haseltine Chafee dined here today, Daughter too spent the day with us, and—but the fact is, I don't feel like writing today.

August 28th, 1864

I believe there is nothing that our better nature needs more absolutely than music, no other art of perfection possesses that strange power of gliding into our every emotion and forming a part of it; poetry, we can only enjoy at times when the spirit is attuned to it, either by calmness, joy, or certain sorts of emotion; but in times of intense grief, who could command one's attention to listen to poetry however beautiful, who could but cast a glance upon the most perfect paintings or even regard the loveliness of flowers, their very brightness of hue would make discord in the heart, & seem unkindly gay; but whose sorrow is not soothed by music, the loud mellow organ peals, with its bewildering solemnity sinks into the soul, mixes with most powerful feelings, calms & sanctifies it. In happiness our joys are expressed & increased by music from the sweet lullaby, sung by a low voiced mother, to the last sad requiem at the grave, music has been unceasingly the soul's true panacea.

"Music that on our spirit gentlier lies
Than tired eyelids upon tired eyes."

Sept. 1st, 1864

Carrie & I went over to Graniteville[1] today, on the way, on the cars an old man took a seat next to me, and began speaking, after a time he told me he had just returned from Richmond, I enquired about the hospitals there, he said that he could not tell me about them because his business had been to one, that his only son had been very ill there, & that the chaplain wrote to tell him of it, & said he would keep on writing to let him know how he was, but he heard nothing more, & he started to go on to enquire himself, concerning him, but finding the enemy in possession of the R.R. he had to return & take the other route, when he reached Richmond after much delay he found that his child had been dead two months, & no one to write him a word; here the great tears rolled down the old man's cheek, "Yes," he said, "the only son I ever had and his mother don't even know it yet." I felt, Oh! so much for the poor old man, he told me the train, the day before had left him & that morning he didn't even wait for his breakfast, but at daylight walked down the road to meet the one we were on, I made him eat half of our lunch, & the rest I tied up & made him put it in his pocket. Oh! this cruel war.

Sept. 26th, 1864

Well here I am home once more after an absence of three weeks in Columbia. I went over to place Mannie at School with the nuns,[2] and then spent my time most delightfully with Rosa Elmore.[3]

We were detained five hours on the cars in going over, during which time a frightful storm arose, but as soon as we reached

1. A small mill village near Aiken in the Edgefield District of South Carolina. The Graniteville Mill was opened in the 1840s by William Gregg.
2. The Ursuline Convent at Valle Crucis in Columbia was founded on Blanding Street in 1858 by nuns from Ireland. It was burned on February 17, 1865, when Sherman's troops entered Columbia.
3. Rosa A. Elmore, age 19, was the daughter of Harriet C. Taylor Elmore, widow of Franklin Harper Elmore (1799–1850), noted lawyer, United States congressman and senator, state legislator, and banker.

Columbia, Albert Elmore[4] soon found us out and had us in the carriage which was waiting for us.

I have really become very much attached to the Elmores, Mrs. Elmore is one of the sweetest persons I ever met, and *all* of them treated me with such great kindness and attention that my time flew by rapidly and charmingly.

Rosa's cousin, Alex. Taylor[5] took me to ride on horseback several times, and was quite attentive to me. She had two soirees while I was with her which were very pleasant, we visited all the pretty surroundings of the place, but I admired Mrs. E.'s more than any I saw. The house was full of lively girls, up to any mischief and fun, and we had no little. Rosa's and my room was the place of rendezvous in night gowns every night, and we acted operas, had statues, comic songs, eating, and all sorts of fun. They had a fine billiard table, & I learned how to play.

By the way, I came away just as Albert E. & I were about to become very great friends, I think. He was away the first week & sick most of the second, but the third we saw a great deal of each other. And just before I left, he was becoming quite—what's the word?

I like him extremely, and he is just as handsome as he well can be, he is devoted to music, I played a good deal for him.

The evening before I left we were all sitting in the piazza, & by degrees everybody left, but Monsieur Albert & myself, we sat there 'till the supper bell rang, then went in. Mr. Frank Elmore[6] looked up during a dead pause in the room full, inquired if *we* had *it* all arranged and wanted to know which side I had cut the lock of hair from my head, &c.

We left at three o'clock in the morning, Albert went to the cars & put me under the care of Capt. Calhoun, who proved a very attentive and pleasant escort, he came in at one of the stations laughing very much and told me that one of his friends whom he

---

4. Albert Elmore, age 20, was the son of Sarah A. Brevard Elmore, widow of Benjamin T. Elmore (1787–1841), older brother of Franklin H. Elmore. Benjamin T. Elmore, noted lawyer, state legislator, state treasurer, and comptroller general, was politically powerful in Richland County politics.
5. Probably a reference to Alexina Taylor, age 22, daughter of William Jesse Taylor. In 1868 Alexina married her cousin, Albert R. Elmore.
6. Frank H. Elmore, age 28, was Albert Elmore's older brother. From 1865 to 1876 he was editor of the *Columbia Phoenix*. In the 1870 census his occupation is listed as lawyer.

had not seen for several years told him that he had no idea that he was married, and was delighted to see his wife & little boy looking so well, pointing to Tommie [della Torre] & me.

Tommie came home with me as Tante is not very well & the care of him is too much for her in Columbia.

Oh my! I enjoyed my visit to Columbia *so* much, I feel a little more at ease away down in my heart, but not satisfied yet, neither will I be until I find out exactly what I do want. I thought whilst at the convent that maybe it was to become a member of that happy community, but I doubt it too.

I met some very pleasant gentlemen in Columbia, but admired little Albert, more than any, begging his tall lordship's pardon for calling him little.

October 15th, 1864

I think really that I am getting to be the worst hand at writing in the world, I write so little of late that when I do attempt a letter my ideas are so thick & few that I only express a few half way, won't do old Journal, now will it, to neglect you so?

Belle & George McDonnald spent a week with me since I wrote last, and Carrie, Tommie & I spent several days at [Rose Hill] with them.

Mary Gregg & Pinckney Bull came down, they were both so much attached to our Tonio, whenever they come here they spend some time at his grave in the garden.

Mrs. Gregg sent up & asked me to help her at her table at a *day fair*, so I went. I however didn't do anything, but in no time eat up $8.00 worth of things if the money hadn't been for the soldiers, I wouldn't have done it.

I hear from Rosa Elmore, she & her brother are much pleased with the gloves I sent him, he has returned to the army. Carrie is in Augusta.

Friendship is a mighty fine thing, but no two ways about it, I enjoy having my own room *once* more to myself, 'mazin', but she is *only* to stay three days, those old ladies have been here now almost a year, when we thought two or three months would be the outside of their stay, *they* were almost utter strangers to Mother & mere acquaintances of Fathers, when they came here, Carrie wrote two letters of entreaty for them to come, & 'twas only on *my* account that Mother consented, for them to come till they could get board somewhere; that, they haven't tried for at all. Wish they would, it keeps us from having *our* friends to stay with us as they have the only guest room, & whenever anybody does come, *I* have to give up mine, besides dividing it all the time,—now I know I'm spiteful, but I don't care, it's true, true, true.

October 31st, 1864

This is my natal day, my twenty-first birthday, and it has proved to me how much love God has placed around me, I expected it to go by only with loving wishes & words, as the times are now harder than they ever have been, but as gifts, the following here given me this morning, a nice foot tub from Fa., and in my plate at the breakfast table, a bond for $1,000 with all its valuable coupons, from Fa. too, and $40.00 from Mother, a most exquisitely embroidered French handkerchief from Mrs. Griswold, a pretty black lace veil from Carrie, two days ago Grandmother gave me a quire of note paper, a box of pins, and a nice pair of shoes, now if this isn't good luck, what is it?

Yes, I'm twenty-one today, pretty old I'm getting, what is to turn up by next birthday, God only knows.

I drove Carrie & Mrs. Griswold to Aiken yesterday, we called on the Huberts, who kept us to dinner. The day was quite agreeable, I almost forgot to record the nice dessert, Mother had for me today, a splendid jellied cake and noble floating island, nice at any time, but now, when common brown sugar is $9.00 a pound, it is an extravagant repast, which we all enjoyed 'mazin.

Nov. 6th, 1864

On the 12th we received news of Uncle John's death, poor Uncle John; & we none of us knew how ill he was, we knew no particulars, but what we do know tells us he has been dead since early in Sept. I do not realize it, it came so suddenly & unexpectedly, and I feel sick at heart.

Dec. 3rd, 1864

On the 22d Nov. we heard of Uncle Peter's [della Torre] death, not one particular of either of these two dear uncles' deaths, and it makes me sick to think of all the accumulated sorrow in our home. Tante is here very sick.

I have been ready to leave home on short notice for some days, as the Yankees under Sherman have been thought to have been marching on Augusta, if so, this section of the country wd. be subject to their raids. Father raised a company of old men & as their Captain, led them to the Savannah river, where it was thought the enemy would cross, to dispute their passage, with other companies.

Many families from Augusta & Aiken have left.

Dec. 26th, 1864

Christmas came and went, not much thought of, the fact is things are rushing along at so terrible a rate, to some fearful climax, that we feel all the time as tho we hadn't time to stop to *think* or *feel*, I *cannot make* myself feel anything, 'twould be hypocrasy to say I am sorrowful, (though I should be, I have cause to be, *every way*, surrounded by death & misfortunes) but I don't stop to think of them, I feel as tho sympathy, sensibility, *all* were suspended during the whirl & rushing of everything, & I put off *everything, all,* until after the result—of what, I know not—

Savannah is taken by Sherman[7] and it can't be long now ere our state is overrun by the enemy. Already in this neighborhood have bands of wicked deserters commenced their work of pillage & destruction. I do not go out unless armed. We are in most fearful times & the end is not yet, tho as things go, our end cannot be far. God may yet help us & I rely on Him and feel nearer to

---

7. Gen. William T. Sherman's famous "March to the Sea," begun a month earlier from Atlanta, had cut a wide swath across the state and had culminated in the occupation of the port city of Savannah on December 21, 1864. The city was virtually without defense following the evacuation of 10,000 militia and regulars under the command of Lt. Gen. William J. Hardee. Mayor Richard Dennis Arnold, therefore, met Sherman on the outskirts of the city and surrendered Savannah, thus avoiding any real fighting.

Him than in my life before. I wish I could feel frightened, anxious—anything, but this *waiting*. I am perfectly astonished at myself. I am the life of the house, & I feel lively & cheerful *all* the time, I do not disguise my feelings, for I cannot affect what I don't feel, neither can I describe what I do feel, unless one word can do it, and that word is—nothing.

Dec. 31st, 1864

The last day of this eventful year is over, tomorrow brings '65, and what will *it* bring? Will this night twelve months find us still possessed of our home? God only knows, God only can help us. 1, 2, 3, 4, 5, 6, 7, 8, 9, 10, 11, 12, the clock has struck, may this be a happy New Year.

1865

Chapter Seven

"Here Come the Yankees": General Kilpatrick's Troops Arrive

January 15th, 1865

Carrie & I went to Augusta on 9th, intending to return the next day, but were detained until yesterday morning, by a dreadful freshet of the river, the City was submerged & persons cd. only venture about the streets in boats; four miles of R.R. washed away, yesterday under cousin Mack's care, we walked two miles at three A.M. to where the car was and returned in a car load of prisoners, I enjoyed the novelty of the freshet and saw many very amusing accidents, the damage done to the City is, however, tremendous. I saw Sumter Mays, he is a handsome, dashing young man.

Feb. 18th, 1865

The Yankees have come & gone. On the 10th Feb. they encamped at Johnstons. The whole of Kilpatrick's forces, they were turned on the country for forage, plunder, & provisions.[1] The first we saw of them was about a dozen of them, dashing thro the gate shouting: "Here come the Yankees, look out now you d——d rebels." A moment after they were in the house, Mother & Grandmother met them at the door, but they didn't listen to a word they tried to say, but said, "Come give us your keys, where

---

1. *The Edgefield Advc. tiser* of February 14, 1865, reported the following: "Early on Thursday morning last, it was announced among us that a large and formidable body of Yankee cavalry, under Kilpatrick, had entered Aiken during the previous night. Refugees and straggling soldiers, passing through from below confirmed this rumor, and added that Kilpatrick was passing on to Graniteville and Vaucluse and would no doubt devastate the whole country." Union cavalry under Gen. Hugh Judson Kilpatrick's command was noted for its lack of order and discipline.

is your liquor? get your gold, get your silver, you old women, hurry yourselves, I say." I had a belt on under my dress, with my revolver, and a bag of bullets, caps & powder in my pocket, they rushed into the room, where all of us ladies were sitting, saying, "Give me your revolvers, d———d you, if we find them, you'd better look out, where are your pistols, we know you've got 'em." I felt it wouldn't do for them to find mine on me, infuriated as they were, so I took Tante's arm, hurried upstairs & threw the revolver between her sheets, hardly I had finished when the door burst open & the room was filled with them, they pulled the bed to pieces, of course.

We all went into the parlor, and by this time there were hundreds of them, in the house, upstairs, in the garret, in every chamber, under the house, in the yard, garden, &c., &c., some singing, shouting, whistling, and Oh, my God, *such cursing*. Both pianos were going at the same time, with axes they broke open every door, drawer, trunk that was locked, smashed a large French mirror, broke pieces of furniture, and flung every piece of clothing, that they didn't carry off, all over the floors, they got some of Fa.'s prettiest paintings and broke bottles of catsup over them, they carried off every piece of silver, every knife, jewel, & particle of possessions in the house & negro houses, every paper, letter, receipt, &c., they flung to the winds, all the roads are strewn with them. Mother and G. M. went among them like brave women, trying to save some few things in vain, at one time a horrid looking ruffian came into the parlor, seeing only women there, he entered shut both doors, & said in an undertone, "You cursed rebels, now empty your pockets." Ah, mon Dieu, mine had my bag of ammunition in it, I rose, & while he was grabbing Miss Hessie's pocket book, I dropped my bag in a corner & flung an old bonnet over it, in my pocket, he found my watch. "Ah," said he, "This is a pretty little watch, now where is the key, & does it go good?" & the villain put his hand on my shoulder, I rose & stood before him, with all possible dignity & he turned away. Then after taking Tante's watch and everybody's money, he walked up to Mother, grinding his teeth & looking her full in the face, said: "Now, you've just *got* to tell me where your gold & silver is buried, I know you've got it, and if you know what's good for yourself & all in this room, you'll tell me where it is." "I have no gold, my silver you have all taken with every other valuable in the house." "That's a d——d lie, now I'll burn your house this minute, if you don't tell me." "I have nothing more to tell, do you think I'd tell a lie?" "I don't know." Then he walked up & down the room cursing, swearing, threatening, & spitting on every side, then finding he could do nothing with us, took Solomon out, put a pistol to his head, saying he would blow his brains out, if he didn't tell. Solomon is as true to us as steel, so are they all, all faithful & friends to us.

About sundown, on the 10th they left off coming here. I then went to ascertain the fate of my revolver, there it was still rolled in the sheets, thrown on the floor with the chaos of clothing. I of course, sent it off. They took every blanket & pillow case & towel, the cases for bags to carry off what they took, & towels for handkerchiefs, they even made the servants get our chemises & tear them up into pocket handkerchiefs for them.

Well the next day, which was Saturday, they came just the same, hundreds of them, one of our villianous neighbors told them that our boys fired the first gun on Sumter, so they said this house was the root of the rebellion & burn it they would, but our good servants & Mother and G. Mother entreated in such a way that they desisted, then they said that they had to arrest and shoot every influential citizen in S.C., every mover of secession, & from the accumulation of wealth, the quantities of food, books & clothes in this house, the finest they had seen in these parts, that they knew Father was wealthy, literary, & influential, & they had heard enough of him, to make an example of him & catch him they would. We have no less than five large libraries of refugees, here, besides our own, & the accumulated clothing & valuables of four separate families, no wonder they found us so rich, & came here so often.

As to provisions, 'tis true, few was so bountifully supplied. We had 7 barrels of fine flour, 300 bushels of corn, 1 barrel & 1 box of nice sugar, &c., &c.

Out of that we have 15 bushels corn, 1 bag flour, 3 hams, they took all the wine & brandy. They had scouts out in every direction looking for Father. Thus passed Saturday, on Sunday morning they burned Uncle & Daughter's home *everything* & every building on their place, even the well, they are here with nothing but their clothes on, in the world, they searched uncle's person.[2] After breakfast, 500 Yankees came here in a body & dispersed over the house & place, carrying off everything they could, they attempted to get into Aiken Saturday morning but were repulsed by Wheeler.[3]

Well, on Saturday night, Father who was encamped in the woods, with the mules, horses & some provisions & one or two of the servants, sent us word that he could not evade the scouts longer & he was going to give himself up to K.ptr. [Gen. Kilpatrick] & demand protection, as a Frenchman, for himself & household, I went down in the swamp to see him & when half way between there & the house saw four Yankees entering the gate, my goodness didn't I run, it was a regular tug between them & me to see who could get to the house first, but I beat in safety, but I never ran so in my life.

Well, after Father went, we were filled with anxiety about him, knowing their threats about him, Oh, we were so frightened for him, when the door opened & a Yankee rushed in with a lit candle, he looked all 'round then ran into every room in the house to look for "that d——d rebel," he then went out saying he'd return during the night to fire the house,—pleasant intelligence— then he & two others asked the servants if there were any young ladies in the house, how old they were & where they slept, during all this I had on blue spectacles & my face muffled up, Carrie too.

When I heard of their questions to the servants I thought that burning the house was nothing; I was almost frantic, I sat up in a corner, without moving or closing my eyes once the whole night. My God! I suffered agony, I trembled *unceasingly* till morning; about eleven o'clock that night, two men went up the back stairs, we heard them walking over head, they went into the

---

2. Pauline's great-aunt and uncle, Dr. and Mrs. J. C. W. McDonald, lived 6 miles from Montmorenci, at Rose Hill. Pauline's father notes in his Journal: "The entire neighborhood was devastated; fences burnt, horses and cattle driven off, provisions taken; all the grist mills burnt except one. Many barns and dwelling houses burnt. All the buildings on Dr. McDonald's place were burnt, 17 in number. Such wanton barbarity has never been seen since the days of the Huns." DeCaradeuc Papers 207, GHS: Journal of Achille DeCaradeuc.

3. Maj. Gen. Joseph Wheeler attacked Kilpatrick's cavalry a short distance beyond Aiken on February 13, 1865. Wheeler's forces had driven Kilpatrick's cavalry as far as Johnston's turnout. There Kilpatrick had taken refuge behind entrenchments where he had some infantry and artillery support. *The Edgefield Advertiser*, February 14, 1865.

room over the parlour (we were in the parlour, of course, all together) and went to bed there, they stayed there all night.

Well, none of us undressed or went to bed for six nights. On Sunday, Mother & Grandmother determined to go out to the camp, to Kilpatrick & ask for protection & for Father's release, they went in the cart with a little blind mule, the only animal they left us, with pieces of yarn for bridle, as they carried off all the harness, &c., during their absence, quantities of Yankees came here, and walked in *every direction* sticking the ground with their swords, feeling for buried things. Wherever the ground was soft they dug, they found all Tante's silver, bonds & jewels, a quantity of provisions,—barrel of wine, one of china, a box of Confederate money & bonds, &c.

Fortunately, the bulk of our silver was sent off.

Mother returned from the camp, bringing Father and William whom they had captured.

Monday morning only a few Yankees came, about ten, I suppose, and then the entire force fell back, not wishing to engage our troops, the R.R., of course, cut & we knew nothing more of them.

Our own soldiers have been coming here constantly, these last two or three days. My goodness, how different they are to the Yankees, the commonest one is as gentle & respectful to us as can be.

Sherman was at Johnstons on Sunday. One dashing looking young officer entered the room where we were sitting on Saturday & Mother said, "Are you an officer, sir?" "I am Madam." "Then, sir, I entreat your protection for my helpless household." "I will, Madam, God knows I am disgusted with all this." He left the room, *we hoped*, to try to check the pillage, he walked into Miss Hessie's room, broke open her trunk and began stuffing his pockets.

They threw a good many shells at this house.

Chapter Eight

Diversion Amidst Defeat:
Parties and Picnics,
The Confederacy Falls

February 19th, 1865

They have completely destroyed the R.R. from Branchville to
Aiken. Charleston has at last fallen into their hands, our forces
evacuated it before a land attack was made, which they could not
have stood.[1]

Sherman marched to Columbia, shelled & almost entirely
burned it before the women & children could be removed. The
convent, was, of course, plundered and burned too, Mannie
returned to us with nothing but the clothes she had on, she had
been living on one lump of cold rice, a day for three days, as the
Yankees destroyed or carried off every particle of provisions they
could find, for six weeks Mannie had not been undressed, they
were turned from the burning convent at twelve o'clock at night,
their only place of refuge being the churchyard, they sat on the
tombstones all night.[2] Father succeeded in getting two mules for
the purpose of going for Mannie, he went to Columbia, but found
she had left the day previous in a train of wagons, he overtook her
at Aiken & they returned together.

I went to Aiken last Monday, spent the day & night at the
Heywards,[3] visited all my friends there & went to the cars to
return home, met Tante in them going to Augusta, she invited me
& I went with her.

---

1. The Confederates evacuated Charleston February 17, 1865, and the Federal
   forces occupied the city the following day.
2. The mother superior of the Ursuline Convent in Columbia had secured from
   Gen. Sherman a guard of protection. It was the guards, however, who began
   the sacking of the convent before the nuns had all left. The students and
   teachers had fled to the Catholic church sanctuary for refuge. DeCaradeuc
   Papers 1497, SHC: Memoirs . . . .
3. The Jonathan Thomas Heywards, parents of Pauline's friend Meta.

I spent the first night with cousin M. the rest of the week with the McDonald's; had a pleasant time.

Gen. Beauregarde's nieces, the Misses Guyol & his son, Capt. Beauregarde called on me twice, the latter, also spent the evening there, he is very handsome, and has easy, finished manners, he sings remarkably well, & dances delightfully, taught me how to waltz, a la New Orleanders. I liked him, beaucoup, but there's an end of him.

Capt. John McDonald was quite attentive to me, I took several promenades with him, &c., but I don't like him, de tout.

I came home yesterday evening.

Saturday, [March] 18th, [1865]

Ah, me! I have caught a famous blue devil, I'm below zero today. I am so different from other people, that when I do go out, I feel lonely in company, I'm so slow, I can't flirt or affect, or be witty or amusing, or in fact, *anything* like anybody else, but I'm too quiet, dull & stupid for anything. I'm entirely disgusted with myself, my face, which folks usually fancy, attracts them towards me, but my face is a story for *it looks* interesting, whereas I am, I suppose, just about as uninteresting & unattractive a person in society as can be found, consequently very disappointing. What do I care for good looks, without a pleasing manner to match, mais helas. I'm getting to dispise that girl whom they call Pauline DeCaradeuc. Well, but I *don't* & *shant* care, & now I feel better in spite of my utter void of spirit.

By the way, I had my fortune told, I'm to marry a man with blue eyes & hair,—to such a devotee to black eyes & hair, that is enough to drive one mad. I trust the blue devil which haunts me, is not significant.

March 22d, 1865

Father returned from Augusta, this morning, where he thinks of getting a house, I hope we will go, for in every point of view I think it advisable.

After dinner I dressed up as an old country woman to deceive Father and sent for him to go out to me in the piazza, but just as

Montmorenci, the DeCaradeuc home near Aiken, South Carolina (courtesy of John Smallbrook Howkins III).

Pauline's grandfather, Jean Baptiste Ursule Laurent DeCaradeuc ("Hercule") (courtesy of Mary DeCaradeuc Bartholomew).

Miniature portraits of Pauline's parents, James Achille DeCaradeuc and Elizabeth Ann della Torre DeCaradeuc, by Achille DeCaradeuc (courtesy of John
Smallbrook Howkins III).

Jacob Guerard Heyward, circa 1861 (courtesy of the Georgia Historical Society).

Guerard's parents, George Cuthbert Heyward and Elizabeth Martha Guerard Heyward (courtesy of Alice Heyward).

James Achille DeCaradeuc (courtesy of Mary DeCaradeuc Bartholomew).

Pauline DeCaradeuc Heyward and Jacob Guerard Heyward, circa 1885 (courtesy of Alice Heyward).

The Heyward Family, 1897. Front row, l. to r:: Elise Heyward Howkins, Guerard Heyward Howkins, Pauline DeCaradeuc Heyward, John Smallbrook Howkins, Jr., Elizabeth Ann della Torre DeCaradeuc, Pauline Overton, Arthur Overton, Nina Heyward Overton. Back row, l. to r.: Dr. John Smallbrook Howkins, Walter Heyward, Frank Heyward, Maude Heyward (courtesy of John Smallbrook Howkins III).

we began our "parlez" a carriage drove up & seeing a handsome young officer therein, I rushed upstairs 'ta fait une toilette' leaving Father slightly bewildered, the officer was Lieut. Hankinson & his mother & sister,[4] they spent the evening, then went off.

April 22d, 1865

Daughter & I went over to Augusta on the 10th for Holy Week, and remained until the 20th, we stayed at the McDonalds, and really I had a very pleasant time, first, the privileges of church & Easter communion, and then dancing, music & amusements of all sorts. We visited the Jewish synagogue and the Methodist meeting, the former impressed me, the latter amused.

Some young men took us on a charming sailing party down the river, it reminded me of similar excursions at Savannah, last year this time.

I met a good many gentlemen, and really, I believe my head is turning back part before with all the compliments I heard, of which were paid me.

Capt. Hooe of Va.[5] I saw a good deal of, as soon as I saw him I was struck with the resemblance to myself, & he the same, in fact everyone remarked how much alike we were, he told Georgie that he had never been so charmed with any lady before & was delighted that I was going to leave Augusta so soon, for he did not wish to see any more of me, as he didn't want to fall in love now while everything is so dark & bewildered. But I ought [not] to commence to write trash & compliments here, after *so much* sense in the book.

Mr. Saussy of Savannah & Mr. Emille Martin of N.O. were the next who pleased *me* most, & whom I *pleased* most, several others too I found amusing & entertaining.

The girls had a charming dance On Easter Monday night, there were about forty-six ladies & gentlemen, I enjoyed it splendidly, in the afternoon two young gentlemen came with Adrienne Guyol to teach us to dance "deux temps." I learned it with very little difficulty, and like it best of all dances.

4. See note 9, chapter 3.
5. Capt. Philip B. Hooe, Assistant Adjutant General, Gen. Montgomery Corse's Brigade.

We attended a sociable at Mrs. Eves' too, which was very agreeable, and also one at the Guyols & we had several impromptu dances at the McDonalds, which were quite charming. At these I really didn't recognize Pauline de Caradeuc in the character of a belle, she has been so long in quiet & retirement, that I almost had forgotten her in society.

Mr. Cohen & I started quite a friendship, the last time I was in Augusta which grew extensively with this visit, he took me to church, &c., and presented me with a lovely box of "Poudre Francais." Sent me "Vanity Fair" which I have been crazy to read, he engaged me to go to the concert next week with him too, but as I'm not there, I suppose I'll not go.

By the way, I must write quite a little episode in every day affairs here. Kate & I were walking up & down under the shade trees on Broad St., where it is cool & quiet, a little servant girl ran up to me with a most exquisite bouquet of white & pink rose buds and said a soldier sent her to give them to me. We asked her who he was, but she didn't know, and as we turned we saw two officers who bowed and turned 'round the corner. That's all of this.

Mr. Saussy came over one morning to teach me how to do hair work, the lesson lasted from nine to one o'clock, & left me an apt scholar. He gave me a nice little machine for making it on.

Yesterday, Mannie, Father & I went to a picnic given at Mr. Benson's farm[6] by the girls of Aiken & the young men. I danced every time but none of the young men were particularly pleasant, the dinner was decidedly the most agreeable feature of the day.

A funny circumstance happened on the car day before yesterday. Daughter & I couldn't get seats in the ladies' car & had to go in the soldiers'. We were in the shade of the door, when three officers came in, and sat ahead of us, one very coolly pulled off his coat, then his vest, then his cravat & collar, & dear knows how much more would have come off, when he turned and saw me; they were all behaving shamefully smoking, drinking, &c., when they discovered us, they seemed terribly abashed & the one in dishabile instantly retired "to dress."

Yesterday, at the picnic, they were there. Dr. Ford, one of them, asked an introduction & apologized, then asked permission

---

6. Probably a reference to L. S. Benson, a landholder in Barnwell County.

to present his friend, Lieut. Brent (the one who undressed himself)
but he couldn't muster resolution enough for the ordeal, until
after dinner, when his heart was warmed, when he was formally
presented, &c., &c.

April 26th, 1865

Ah, Mon Dieu! what news, what terrific bewildering news;
Can it be true? is the Confederacy subjugated? Have the chivalry
of the South given their lives in vain?

All our brave Generals, unequalled soldiers, my own gallant
Brothers, was it for this that you died? subjugation! Never! God
will raise us yet.

Lee, Robert E. Lee, the General of the age, has capitulated,
with his army,[7] report says the men refused to leave Va. and, so,
outnumbered as they were, it was impossible to remain there,
however it is, our cause is lost, lost, men from the remaining
remnant of the army have flung down arms and returned home.

Lincoln was at the theater on the evening of the 12th [April 14].
Suddenly a man sprang into his box, shot him thro the head,
flung the pistol into the crowd, saying "Sic semper tyranis," "the
South is avenged," he sprang into the pit, rushed across the stage
and disappeared thro the green room, leaving the monster dying.

The same night a man made his way into Seward's apartment & stabbed him & his son, it is thought the former is mortally
wounded. God grant it.[8]

We have now an armistice, and arrangements for peace are
going on, upon what terms God only knows; persons think the
U.S. are in a difficulty with Europe and are trying to gain us back
upon any terms, before launching into another war.

Oh, could we have held out a little longer.

Johnston too has surrendered his army,[9] many think the war
is over, and we are subjugated entirely, I won't believe that.

7. On April 9, 1865, Gen. Robert E. Lee surrendered the Army of Northern
   Virginia to Gen. Ulysses S. Grant at Appomattox, Virginia.
8. On the same evening of John Wilkes Booth's assassination of President Lincoln, Lewis Paine, a former Confederate guerilla, made an unsuccessful attempt
   on the life of Secretary of State William Henry Seward.
9. Although Gen. Joseph E. Johnston and Gen. William T. Sherman met April
   17, 1865, near Durham Station, North Carolina, to negotiate a peace settlement, the formal surrender of Johnston's army did not take place until May 3.

Mr. Davis has gone to the trans Mississippi, it is thought to try and rally, and continue the war, every man is a traitor & coward who doesn't go with him, & fight to the death to keep us from this disgraceful reunion.[10]

I *won't* believe our cause is lost, so far we are only outnumbered, *in every* fair fight we have been victorious for four years, and it was not, it could not have been for this—never—God who is justice, will accept the sacrifice of the lives of the Chivalry of the South, and give their land its own proud place among nations.

Oh! such a trying time, we have been cut off from all regular news, and chance brings us such conflicting & distracting rumors every day, that it is horrible to live.

Wheeler's stragglers went to Augusta "en masse" on May 1st, broke open all public stores, &c., and carried off everything they could find, they were about burning down the City itself, when Gen. Wright[11] arrived with some troops, drew them up in line of battle on Broad St. made them (the mob) a stump speech, &c. and checked them, they had, however, behaved in a terrifying way, and stolen $300,000 worth of Government clothes alone, several of the most daring men were shot by private persons in defending their property. Mr. William McDonald lost all his clothes, stores, &c. & horses from his farm, he killed a man too.

There was to have been an insurrection of the Negroes in Augusta & Charleston this week, both were betrayed & stopped in time.

Father, Tante, Mannie & I went over to Augusta yesterday on business. I carried some splendid strawberries for friends there, one basket I sent to Adrienne Guyol, by Joe. I saw Capt. Hooe & Emille Martin standing at the opposite corner talking, they asked Joe if I wasn't Miss P. de C. I went in to see the MacD.'s & carry them some berries too, about five minutes after, Capt. H. & E. M.

---

10. President Jefferson Davis was captured in the vicinity of Irwinville, Georgia, May 10, 1865, and imprisoned for two years at Fort Monroe, Virginia.

    Lt. Gen. E. Kirby Smith, who commanded the Trans-Mississippi Department, was the last Confederate general to accept defeat. His department was surrendered in his name by Lt. Gen. Simon B. Buckner at New Orleans May 26, 1865.

11. Maj. Gen. Ambrose Ransom Wright, a Georgian, had been assigned to Georgia on November 26, 1864.

called there too & paid a long visit. E. M. who is a paroled prisoner, returns today to N. O. his home, he has to walk 90 miles, as the R. R. is not remade yet. Capt. H. leaves for trans. Mississippi this week, he is dreadfully distressed about the times.

They both evinced great pleasure in seeing me, & took very touching farewells. I saw a good many of my friends.

Mr. Saussy has begged Miss Maggie to bring him down here, but now I suppose no one would care to go about, at least, they ought not to.

There was a large picnic given at Mr. Benson's farm on Tuesday, to which I was invited, I of course, never thought of going, *now*, that the country for which I have worked, suffered, & prayed for, for four years has met with the greatest of all trials, could I have the heart to dance, & go to pleasure parties—*What a mockery*!

The young men sent a buggy here for me, instead of hanging their disgraced heads over their paroles, or rallying on to trans. Miss., they remain to dance & be merry over the death of their country, shame! shame!—of course, I sent their buggy back to them empty!

May 15th, 1865

There is no use in trying to delude myself any longer, our men have behaved disgracefully, have deserted, straggled & everything else. Johnston himself seems to have acted treacherously, and Pres. Davis was betrayed to the enemy whilst going to the trans. Miss., he was captured and sent to Savannah.

The Yankees are undisputed masters of this betrayed land, and their iron heel is already pressed upon the conquered, it serves us right, for all the disgraceful conduct. All I want is to leave this vile place, to go to some other country. I hate everything here, and Davis—the purest patriot, the greatest statesman, and wisest administrator that ever lived, is the man I'm sorry for. Would to God, I could die to save him from sorrow, and the humiliations which are to be heaped upon his great soul.

Nothing can express what I feel for my own noble President. Yes! now indeed has come the end.

May 16th, 1865

Col. Hatch[12] came from Charleston two days ago & spent a night with us, he is a Yankee at heart & I hate him.

Two nights ago Capt. Conner[13] came in, he came on from Johnston's army, to see Brother, never having heard of his death; he was in prison with him, and frequently my dear Brother had told me of him, he remained with us two nights and left this morning, he is going to leave this country for South America, we *all* want to go. God speed us.

The negroes are all freed in Augusta.

Capt. Milledge has gone on to Va. to bring back his bride (Miss Nannie Robertson). Always what I predict, comes to pass.

The Yankees with a vileness consistent with their entire conduct, and endeavoring to cast the odium (?) of their leading Devil's death (Lincoln) upon Pres. Davis. They will hang him, I know, but it is not in the power of man or Devil, to cast one shade, on the spotless purity of that brilliant star. God bless him!

Hundreds of soldiers go up daily for their paroles.

Phoebe Gibbes spent last week here. Ah! how I wish I had pleasing manners like other people. I don't know a single soul like myself.

May 28th, 1865

Robbie & Phoebe Gibbes spent last week here with us, he returned from the army about ten days ago, it really amused me very much, his playing the devoted to me. The other evening I had to put on quite *elderly airs* to prevent him from making a ninnie of himself. But he is a good fellow as ever lived, & was a dear friend of Tonio's and I love him very much for that.

Julia [Parrott] also, spent most of the week with Mannie, and as usual, I was called upon to invent amusement for them all; I gave them all several dancing lessons, playing lots of games,

---

12. Probably Col. Lewis M. Hatch, State Engineer, Department Headquarters, South Carolina, Georgia, and Florida.
13. Capt. W. G. Conner, Jeff Davis Legion, was reported captured while detached from his company on picket by Brig. Gen. J. E. B. Stuart in a report dated May 13, 1862. Orders for his exchange were issued from Washington on August 27, 1862. *OR*, I, 11, pt. 2, pp. 444–45; *OR*, II, 4, p. 442.

walked, talked & slept & made them otherwise agreeable to themselves & me. Robbie, I taught two duets, he taught me two songs,
and I gave him one or two French lessons, which he professed to
enjoy amazingly, really I was quite instructive.

Mr. Ryan came down two days ago, and will remain a few
more days, with us. Daughter & Uncle came over to Mass before
breakfast, this morning. Mannie returned home with R. & P.
yesterday evening.

June 2d, 1865

The anniversary of my poor friend George's death. Mr. Ryan
still being with us, I got Mother, to have Mass offered for the
repose of his soul. My poor brave friend, *now* I would not recall
you if I could, to the country now disgraced and conquered, for
which you died. No our Chivalry is dead, and in that happy land
"dominut in sommo pacis."

June 17th, 1865

Father returned from Augusta last night, bringing with him,
Mr. Freeman, a young Virginian, who is very handsome and
exceedingly pleasant, as are all Virginians, he remained 'till this
morning, when he started to walk to Chston. I took a great fancy
to him, there is something so genuine in him, I don't know what it
is. I like him 'mazin.

We are all so anxious to go to Brazil, things are becoming
more & more practicable too, thank God.

June 18th, 1865

I went to Aiken on the train this morning to spend the day
with the Parrotts.[14] Tom Heyward[15] met me at the depot and

---

14. Julia, Fannie, Abner Flint, and William W. Parrott were friends of the
DeCaradeuc sisters. Flint Parrott was a member of Company H., 14th South
Carolina Regiment, McGowan's Brigade; he had been wounded at Cold Har-
bor June 1862 and was discharged January 1863. *Cemetery Inscriptions, Aiken
County,* WPA Project, 1949; Agatha A. Woodson, Confederate Scrapbook.
15. Thomas Josias Heyward, cousin of Guerard, was the son of Mr. and Mrs.
Jonathan Thomas Heyward and the brother of Pauline's friend Meta Heyward.

escorted me to their house, spent a pleasant day there; in the afternoon, Flint Parrott escorted me to the Heywards where Meta was expecting me, I enjoyed my visit to her very much. Tom Heyward begged me to put his name down on the list of recruits for Brazil, so did Flint & Major Dickson. T. H. went with me down to the depot to see me on the returning train, just as we reached there, a regiment of Negroes arrived, there were hundreds of their color there to welcome them, and Mon Dieu! what yells, shouts & frantic gestures they made to evince their joy & excitement. They were the first black troops I ever saw, I felt every imaginable emotion upon seeing them, they, who two or three months ago were our respectful slaves, were there as impertinent as possible, pushing & jostling us about, one Negro woman gave me a pinch on my arm, I did not notice it, as they are supported in every wrong, nor did I tell Mr. Heyward, to add to the fury and humiliation he must have felt, it was all like a pandemonium of black demons, so intense was the noise & confusion. T. H. & his father were on each side of me, and put me in the conductor's car. Tom told me he would come down to see me tomorrow morning to get me to play for him. He & Meta pressed me warmly to stay until tomorrow, when he would drive me home in a spring wagon.

The Parrots begged me also to stay & Flint would drive me home in his ambulance. They made me promise to spend next week there.

June 25th, 1865

Col. Dan Hamilton[16] came here on the 23d and remained with us yesterday, he is a very pleasant man and gave us some charming accounts of scenes of the war, which he passed thro. He says however that Gen. Hampton[17] is not going to Brazil as reported; he, Col. H., leaves shortly for Texas, no one can live here now, in any peace, with our slaves over us for masters.

---

16. Col. D. H. Hamilton, First South Carolina Volunteers, had been made colonel of the First Regiment, Gregg's (later McGowan's) Brigade.
17. Lt. Gen. Wade Hampton remained in his native South Carolina and was elected governor in 1876 and 1878. He later served in the United States Senate until 1891.

June 29th, 1865

Well, old Journal, since our last meeting, I have passed thro so many scenes and emotions, how shall I tell you all? simply by commencing at the beginning and stopping at the end, so now for it.

On 27th while we were at dinner, two Yankee soldiers walked in and asked father for some brandy, he told them he had none to spare; they insisted, father persisted, until they said they would go down to the wine cellar & look for themselves, Father went with them, they were both armed with muskets & revolvers, and when they found that there was none there, they said they would search the house, father told them that would be an outrage upon his family that he would not allow, and he would resist any such act.

When he said that the one behind him struck him over the head with his musket, which being so wholly unexpected, knocked him down, then they fell on him and kicked him and knocked him with their guns until he was insensible, the negroes all ran to his assistance, but they shot at them, and threatened to kill them, if they dared to render any aid. They then called us and told us Father was killed, we all rushed down to the cellar terror stricken and saw him lying bleeding on the ground, we raised him & revived him, then I made Joe saddle the horse for me to go imme-diately to headquarters and bring a guard to arrest the villians, but one of them stood in front of the horse with his revolver cocked saying he'd kill anyone who attempted to mount. Then they searched the entire house, stole all the brandy and tobacco and left, we then sent for the Dr. [Coffin], and in a short time, he & his two sons, Amo & Charles came down, he said none of Father's bones were broken, and that his bruises internally & externally, though very painful, were not serious.

After all this my first thought was for redress, so I got up at daylight the next morning, and went to Augusta to Gen. Molineaux.[18] At Aiken, I saw the commander there & got him to

18. Brevet Brig. Gen. Edward L. Molineux was in command of a brigade of the 19th Corps, which was sent in early May 1865 to garrison Augusta. *OR*, I, 49, pt. 2, p. 603.

send a guard to protect the place as the villians said they were going to return. I went to Gen. M. Mr. Heyward went with me, and I had an interview of about an hour and a half, he did not seem inclined to give me what I wanted at first, but I was determined to get both a guard, and to have the men arrested & punished, so I telegraphed to Columbia to have them arrested as soon as they reached there, if they had already left Johnstons, and if still there, he gave me a letter to Capt. Jackson in Aiken, ordering their arrest at once, he also gave me a guard. He told me that in order to have them identified it would be necessary for me to go to Columbia, I told him, "Certainly I would go, that was no difficulty by any means." Then he asked me if we thought those men had been sent here . . . [illegible] I told him yes, by the same who sent the raiders here last winter with the story that my Brother had fired the first gun on Sumter, for these men said the same thing and vowed they would have three-fold vengeance. "Ah," said Gen. M., "And so your Brother fired the first gun on Sumter, did he?" "Sir," I replied, "it is with the utmost regret that I am forced to say that my Brother did not have that honor." I told him the cowardly villians said they had authority to take liquor from any house, which had it. "That," he said, "is a lie." "I was quite aware of that, Sir, coming as it did from Federal soldiers," I answered.

I wd. not have spoken as I did, had he been more polite, but he kept his cigar in his mouth the whole time, which rudeness provoked me at first, and his manner was so nonchalant.

Just as I left, an acquaintance of mine, who knows him very well, went in to see him, he told her he admired me very much, that as soon as he heard me speak, he knew I was a S. Carolinian, and he tried his best to excite me, and make me lose my dignity; wherein he failed signally.—Mais assez de cela.

At the Aiken depot, Amo Coffin was waiting for me and drove me home, that I might not come so far with no protection, but Joe's, he slept here last night, and returned this morning.

What Nellie Redmond told me last summer *is true*, now what a romantic struggle between love & religion, I could have, if the affair were only mutual; but as it is, I rather dislike than otherwise, and feel quite unconcerned.

The guard from Aiken, was of Negro troops, they remained here all day, no white Yankees came either.[19]

July 9th, 1865

I went over to Augusta on the 5th, with Mannie to have her teeth extracted. This painful operation, which has been hanging over her all her life, is at last over, she had fourteen drawn one day & fourteen the next, the dentist, Dr. Holland, procured a physician to give her chloroform, she could not, however, get entirely under its influence and suffered terribly. I suffered greatly too, from seeing her so tried, but it is over now, and I don't like to even think of it. She will have an artificial set put in, in two weeks.

After it was all over, I had quite a pleasant time in A[ugusta],—Took one moonlight walk with Mr. Dutcher, whom I actually hate. The next evening Mr. Cole took me to an exhibition, on the way he began abusing our immortal President Davis, of course, I took his part, he requested me to allow him to change my opinion, I granted his request, but all he gave or anyone else can say, will only increase my admiration, my adoration for the greatest man of the age,—he vexed me,—when we reached the hall he began abusing the Jews, saying, "what an antipathy he had for them, what a low, cunning, mean people they are, and how in Charleston to be seen with a Jewess, was enough to stamp one, &c., &c." I never said a word, but after the exhibition was over, and we went on the street, I said, "Now, Mr. Cole, you have tried to alter my opinion about Mr. Davis, allow me to endeavor to change yours respecting the Jews." "Certainly," he said, "it will be a pleasure to listen to you." "Well, then," I went on, "You Christians are all most unkindly prejudiced against us Jews, which is—" "In heaven's name, are you a Jewess, m'am?" "I am sir." He

19. The town of Aiken was garrisoned for a time by Negro troops. The following is an account by Achille DeCaradeuc: "Rob. Gibbes near Aiken was beaten by a negro who claimed possession of Mrs. G.'s land and the entire crop upon it, cultivated by said negro upon shares with his former mistress. Negro soldiers were sent to arrest R. G. who was obliged to flee and conceal himself. These negros finally revolted against their officers and were withdrawn from Aiken and replaced by a company of Germans who were quiet and well behaved." DeCaradeuc Papers 207, GHS: Journal. . . .

was perfectly speechless, stopped short in the street, and looked me full in the face,—I quietly stopped too, but upon venturing to return his gaze, there was so much consternation and alarm in every feature, that I could not act my part, my gravity vanished, and I shook with laughter, he said, "*Oh*—you're not a Jewess, and I must say thank God for it, for I never felt so terrible in my life." Thus I gave him a lesson, & avenged myself for what he said of President Davis. The next evening, I met him at a sociable, he was quite devoted to me, he said that when he stopped and looked at me in the moonlight, he thought I looked like a Jewess, and he wanted the ground to open and swallow him.

We returned home yesterday.

July 13th, 1865

Yesterday, I went to a picnic given at Mr. Benson's farm, none of the gentlemen were in any way uncommon, and I did not enjoy it much, altho I danced every dance, and as usual received a plenty of attention.

Why do I always inspire *general* admiration, it is the same thing every where I go, I would much rather, a great deal, have but one or two admirers at a party, &c., and let them be agreeable and devoted, instead of having a little bit of *everybody's* attention. I consider myself very unfortunate in this respect.

I promised to spend part of next week with Julia Parrott, let's wait and see what's next.

Capt. Milledge, they say, has married for money, his bride possessing $100,000 in *gold*. I hear she is very ugly, I always thought he'd marry a fortune or—a beauty.

Chapter Nine

Belles and Beaux:
"In Love at Last"

August 12th, 1865

Amelia & Belle McDonald brought their beaux down and spent a week, while here, Mr. Benson gave a dinner party to which we went, 'twas a delightful one, there I met Mr. Guerard Heyward,[1] my new summer friend. He & Mr. B. spent the next day with us, and on table rock, we began quite a desperate flirtation, which progressed rapidly. The day was a charming one, the next evening we were invited to a sociable at Mrs. Schwartz's,[2] we went, and on the way, met Monsieur Guerard, who handed me a poem, which he had just composed for me, the sociable passed off very pleasantly, he & I sat in the moonlight, nearly the whole time, we started to carry on the flirtation, but turned it into friendship, and amused each other famously.

I returned home on Monday; on Tuesday I went back to a surprise party at Fannie Parrotts, of course, little G. was there, and all devotion, we sat in the moonlight again, entertaining each other most of the evening, he said lots of sweet speeches and we had a gay time of it, I received plenty of attention, had a plenty of fun, when we went to bed the sun was shining.

The next evening we went to Mary Williams', G. escorted me there, and was as usual devoted, this evening the goose spoke of changing our friendship into sweethearts, but I'd rather have my fun a little longer; of course, as there was moonlight, we found ourselves seated out in it, &c., &c.

The next morning I left on the cars, he went to see me off.

---

1. Lt. J. G. Heyward, Co. I., First South Carolina Artillery, in operations on Morris Island, 10 July 1863, was reported wounded and taken prisoner. He remained in prison on Johnson's Island (Ohio) until the war's end. *OR*, I, 28, pt. 1, pp. 526–27.
2. Dr. and Mrs. U. B. Schwartz of Aiken.

I met Phoebe Gibbes there who came down with me. We took a touching farewell, and that's the end of him for the present, I hope.

August 20th, 1865

I went over to Augusta, a few days ago, with Mannie, on the way home, at the Aiken depot, some of the girls and young men met me, to try and persuade me to get out & remain for a party next evening, this I couldn't do however. G. H. came in the car & remained talking until it moved off, filled my handkerchief with sugar plums, &c., then left. The next day he brought a buggy down to take me to the party, we went off, and the most terrific storm overtook us,—open buggy—new hat—famous! too much rain for the party, so 'twas postponed 'till next evening. Mr. H. on the way presented me with a lovely little cross, which he carved out of gutta percha, in prison, prettily mounted, 'tis very pretty.

The evening of the party I looked my very best purposely, and consequently had as much homage as I could want & a nice time. G. H. was all devotion, said everything sweet & soft in the language. I'm having my own fun too, sometimes I'm kindness & smiles & delight & sometimes I make him believe I'm quizzing him, which is the truth for my heart is intact, thank goodness; & he don't bother my head much. We had two talks in the piazza, terribly long ones, & he hovered around me the rest of the time.

Gov. [Rob.] Barnwell Rhett[3] was introduced to me, the fire-eating editor of the Mercury; did nothing but quarrel about Mr. Davis, *my* immortal hero; *his* deadly enemy, enjoyed myself a good deal, next day, I spent with Meta Heyward. G. called in the afternoon, he & Mr. Gignilliat went to the cars with me, *he* came in & had a long chat before we left.

---

3. "Gov." is undoubtedly an error in transcription. The reference is to Robert Barnwell Rhett, Jr., editor of the Charleston *Mercury*, a radical proslavery, prosecessionist newspaper, considered one of the most caustically anti-administration papers in the Confederacy. He was the son of Robert Barnwell Rhett, Sr., who had taken John C. Calhoun's Senate seat in 1837–49. The senior Rhett was called the "Father of Secession," and was a frequent critic of Jefferson Davis during the war. He later opposed reconstruction, opting for an independent southern confederation.

Mary Williams told me that Lizzie Coffin told her, that Amo had nearly been distracted between his love for his religion & myself, it amuses me *now*, tho! it didn't *once*, he keeps pretty clear of me. My faith has kept back a good many from seriousness; John Milledge last summer couldn't abide it, & I know it's the hardest nut for G. H. to crack, nevertheless, all this only increases my ardent love for it.

Sept. 10th, 1865

I haven't written here for a long while, for various reasons. Meta Heyward came out & spent week before last with me, and I returned last week & remained with her 'till last night. I spent a very pleasant time. G. H. came down to the train to meet us, & spent the evening at Meta's.

Next morning he sent me a delicious cup of chocolate, quite a rarity these times. I was playing invalid; that evening we took a moonlight walk. Next morning he came in at nine o'clock & left at two. That evening he called for me in a buggy, we went out to see Phoebe Gibbes . . . [illegible]

Next morning, came at nine o'clock, stayed 'till two, *so* tiresome. That evening came again! stayed 'till near eleven. Next morning a beautiful little silver waiter, with the daintiest little lunch in the world & little note to match, came in. That evening he came 'round & we all went to a small party. I felt very unwell & couldn't enjoy myself at all, some little coldness passed between us, quite a damper.

Next morning he came for a few minutes, had no opportunity of explaining, so went off, still in coldness, sent me his autograph album, kept in prison to look at, with the stiffest sort of a note, asking me to write my name in it, I wrote a note, just as stiff, refusing. Didn't come near me all day, my last day too. In the afternoon, I left on the cars, he was at the depot, came up, *hoped*, we parted as friends in a very significant way; remained with me 'till train left but had no opportunity for explaining away misunderstanding, if there were any, as Mr. Gignilliat, Meta, Tom Heyward & Mr. McDonald were all with me.

So now my poor little friend what will you do? I'm quite curious to know.

Amo alarmed me, by visiting me & appeared quite charmed.
Tom Heyward is a splendid fellow, he came down with me, on
the train, begged me to write his name on the list of my truest
friends & greatest admirers. He & I have become fast friends, I
hope.

Mr. Gignilliat, too, was very kind to me, he & I carried on a
regular flirtation, had a very nice time, but am sorry for the
misunderstanding (?) with my friend. I can't write half of his
devotion here, or his grateful & delicate attentions.

Will we make up or not? & do I care?

Sept. 15th, 1865

Mrs. Coffin is spending a week with us, I dressed up as an old
woman, after tea, for her amusement, made a fright of myself,
went 'round thro the front gate, knocked & came in. Two figures
followed, unseen by me, & while I was talking like an old cracker,
completely deceiving Mrs. C., we heard a light tap on the door,
Mannie asked, "Well, what do you want?" the answer was, "Mr.
Heyward has called," sure enough, there were G. & Tom standing
in the door. I forgot my character & rushed upstairs full tilt. They
enjoyed the catch greatly. Plague take it! Tom just devoted himself so terribly to me, that I hardly said a word to my friend,
consequently, as we have made no explanation of our coldness,
&c., I suppose we are still *trop froid.*

I begin to feel right concerned about it, he brought me a piece
of music tonight. Wish I could only have a good long talk with
him by myself & fix everything right again, a very few words wd.
do it—plague take Tom.

Sept. 16th, 1865

Aunt Ada arrived unexpectedly tonight, it recalls great sadness. She looks very beautifully.

I wonder if my friend & I will ever really make up! don't care,
after all if we don't.

Sept. 18th, 1865

This afternoon, G. & T. & Mary Williams & Fannie Simmons, came down in a pelting rain, stayed all night, had a mighty nice time. G. & I made up finely, exchanged rings as a token of— friendship, & had a long talk in the piazza.

Sept. 20th, 1865

Went up to a party given at Mrs. Coffin's, I went in the morning, found G. H. there, he stayed 'till two o'cl. Enjoyed party very much. G. was as usual devoted, he presented me with a most lovely white crane fan, he shot the bird. Amo did not join the party 'till very late, danced once with me, then retired to his room, he amuses me very much, tho I don't understand him, in the dance I noticed his hands were trembling whenever we turned, oh, bien! I can't help it. Mrs. C. put her arms 'round me, kissed me & said, "Oh! Paul, if you would only be my daughter." I grinned in her face & left.

The next morning G. came 'round of course. We had to talk in whispers, as Dr. C. was very ill, we had a long talk too, he brought his autograph album for me to write my name in. I did it this time. He also brought me a lovely ring, which he made in prison, put it on my hand, begging me to wear it,—I promised to do so for a little while, he also begged me to accept some pressed moss, which he fixed in prison, dear only knows what all he don't want me to accept!

In the afternoon, I returned on the train, Lizzie, Mary, Charlie & Amo walked to the train with me. G. was there with a rose bud for me. Amo, who had been by my side, immediately gave way as G. approached, the latter came in the car & sat there 'till it moved off. Amo stood up outside of the window. Heigh, Ho!

Sept. 21st, 1865

Amo came down to hunt this morning, came at 8 o'cl. hunted 'till eleven, then read poetry to me & had a religious controversy, a real fine one this time, & I played on the piano for him, 'till dinner time. In the afternoon he drove Aunt Ada & me to the cars,

& then went home, he left his gun & dog, for us to take care of. Mrs. Coffin told Mother that Amo was my greatest admirer, sorry it is not *now* mutual, *far* from it. Ah, me!

Sept. 30th, 1865

Mary W. & Lizzie & Charlie Coffin spent several days with me; we, with Aunt Ada's assistance, had a gay time of it. Dear me! but I have taken a pretty conspicuous part in a game of amusement for those girls, *revenge for myself*; right or wrong, I intend leaving my own feelings aside and dive into it in good heart, in time I will tell you; for the present, it is enough that I have been deceived in the truth & candour of one whom I esteemed; perhaps I ought to let things drop just so, but *no, no*, I consented to act my part in the game, and I *will* do it most thoroughly—*now* see if I don't.

Oct. 16th, 1865

Well, old Journal, let me tell you a secret, or, rather it is now no longer a secret—for everybody knows; you could never guess—for I am engaged to be married, in love, at last, yes positively & terribly in love, I confess it, but with the dearest, sweetest & best of good fellows, no one could help loving him, I only found out how truly I loved him, when he told me of his, for before, I was afraid of my own heart's suspecting its own feelings.

I am happy, happy from morn to night.

My first love too; for of all who have before spoken to me of love, I have never felt one flutter in my heart equal to its very tinyest throbs now. And now, I am afraid I am only too happy. I love & am loved too much, but I haven't told you who *he* is, no other than that scamp Guerard Heyward, God bless him, God bless him. Mon Dieu!! & My conspiring!

Dec. 3d, 1865

All this time has passed so happily that I have not felt like recording it, Guerard, my own love, has been devoted to me, I believe he loves me as much as I love him, and Heaven knows how *entirely* that is.

Whenever I feel *bad*, I just think of him, "Gentle & brave & generous" as he is & I feel tranquilized & *SUperlatively* happy, his parents came to see me, dear heart! I was in a flurry, but I can generally "hide my scare."

Guerard went to town the other day to get into business. I think only of him, and really I believe my love increases every day, the mails are cruelly irregular, but we write often, still I miss him every hour.

Spent two days with Lizzie C. Amo was more kind, more attentive than he has been since lang syne.

Lizzie & I understand each other well, we are not in love with each other, tho will continue to be friends. Amo gave me a beautiful, but sad poem, one of his own.

When I came home, I found a *love letter of the first water* awaiting me, from—

My old hero, Major Buford, now living out West, he has written me frequently, tho for some months, I never answered his letters, which are always, however beautiful & respectful, he alludes to many which I have not received too, but my friend you are, I am thankful to say, "*too late*, too late, ye cannot enter now," I wrote him a regular damper. I'll make Guerard, my darling, laugh at it when I see him.

1866

Chapter Ten

Guerard Heyward:
"My Own True Love"

Jan. 2d, 1866

Attended two very pleasant parties in Aiken, lately, stay at the Coffins now nearly always. Amo translated for me one of my favorite poems, from Lamartine. Ah, me! another letter from Buford, this time entreating for encouragement to come on & plead his cause in person, I didn't show this one to Mother, but burnt it, Fa wants to know what gentlemen writes me from Memphis, as he brought both letters to me. I will write him once more & this time I'll wager he'll not venture to write me in this strain again.

Jan. 19th, 1866

I have just written to Guerard, time and absence but add to my love.

I went over to see Nellie & Mel [Redmond], spent twelve delightful days with them at their home near Berzelia, Ga. Mr. Franklin & Hugh Colquitt were there too. Mel bent on making the latter & myself friends called us most solemnly into the parlour, placed my hand in his, made us vow eternal friendship, which he sealed with a kiss on my hand, they are soon to marry, and are a splendid couple every inch of them, he can't compare with my Guerard, oh, no!

We went to town and stayed four days at Maj. & Mrs. Conner's, two gay and charming folks from N. O. great friends of the Redmonds, they gave us a gay time. We attended the ball of the season while there, which was brilliant. There I had the only thing that could do to test my love for Guerard & prove that it is complete & immense.

I was dancing & looking up saw Joe Cumming[1] as vis-a-vis, his large black eyes fixed on me, he immediately crossed over and greeted me cordially, four years ago in the same hall we met, he remembered all our conversations, & all the incidents of that ball. When I looked into his eyes a pair of keen grey ones, shone thro my heart telling me I *never, never,* loved any but them, my own Guerards, & I knew it well by my unconcern, this is *all* I wanted, & I'm happier, etc., than ever.

Joe put his name on my card for three waltzes and supper, and I enjoyed a friendly chat first rate, when he saw me leaving he, — but fudge —.

Dr. Habersham[2] played the devoted to me, and begged me to allow him to come down here next week & bring some new music & his flute to play with me.

The plagued Joe Milledge has told him of my engagement by now, so I reckon the Dr. will not trouble himself any further. A propos of Capt. Jack [Milledge], Mel [Redmond] was always his confident, she told me as *information* that he never loved any woman but me, but meant to convert me before marrying me, just like his conceit and impudence.

This seems to be a chapter on beaux so I might as well go on. Roland Steiner of yore, learning I was in town, called one morning, took me to walk that evening, stayed 'till eleven that night, took me to church next morning, came again that evening, remained 'till near twelve, came at nine next day and remained until dinner time, when *we* left Augusta. Now what did we talk about, why this, for two years I've never laid eyes on him, he gave himself up to dissipation in extreme, & was truly wicked, he resolved to reform and came down here to see me in his buggy, got lost, went back to ask Mr. Henry to come with him, Mr. H. told him if he dared to attempt seeing me, he wd. write Father such a letter as would cause him to close the doors on him forever; he says, then he felt the truth of this, & his own guilt & unworthiness, and despair sent him back to his evil ways; on the 1st of this Jan. he

---

1. Joseph B. Cumming, age 24, was a lawyer in Augusta.
2. This probably is a reference to Dr. Joseph Clay Habersham (1830–1881), who served during the war as surgeon of the 25th Georgia Regiment and later became health officer of Savannah and president of the Georgia Medical Society. Joseph Clay Habersham Paper 340, GHS.

says he resolved to reform and hearing I was once more in Augusta, believed God sent me to exert over him the influence he needed to carry out his resolves, he was so emphatic & impulsive he alarmed me, he carried me to his sisters' grave and told me there, that there was no use to struggle with fate, that he & I were decreed to be the best of friends, that he felt it, I had been the one object of his life; that he knew & understood me instinctively; he was impelled to speak; resistance was folly, he knew it was bad taste to speak to me, from my own home, but he could not help it, and entreated me to tell him at once that he could end friendship and be my lover. I was frightened by his impetuosity, but calmly told him that I would always be his friend, willing to aid & support him & uphold him in his good resolutions, but further than that was utterly impossible. He said, "Yes, I understand, I've told you my crimes and you could never forgive or forget." I told him I had already done both, & respected him for his reformation. I told him of my engagement, excited as he was, I had to. His confidence in his belief that Providence sent me as his good angel was so great, that this seemed to stun him for awhile, then he stood before me with a burst of eloquence such as I never heard.

Roland is the most talented as well as the most unfortunate young man in Augusta, finely educated, inheriting his father's intellect. I was unusually excited & scarcely kept from crying; but I knew well enough the value of my calmness & preserved it,—he felt—& we went back to Mr. R.'s.

I was to return home the next day & he to leave for Jefferson, he however waited and went to meet me at the depot, I did not go 'till day after, when he postponed again to meet me, took me to the train in his buggy, entreated me to re-establish my friendship, to continue my "pure & holy influence" & help him still. Of course, I consented, he gave me a beautiful poem of his own, brought a quantity of books for me to read, and petitioned to be allowed to come down for them himself next Friday. I never saw such repentance & despair as he shows. I feel very sorry for him if he acts up to what he says. I am very glad he has gone into society again, he is so witty & smart that the girls welcome him again. I will not write this to my darling as it might worry him on paper when if I *tell* him, I'm sure of his countenance.

In Augusta, we attended several dances which were all pleasant, & I enjoyed also, several nice rides.

My old friend Paul Hayne,[3] I saw much of, we were to correspond. Dr. Habersham asked me if I had seen my admired Gen.
Hood[4] lately, I told him I never had seen him to my knowledge, he
said "yes I had, for one day I was at the cars, on horseback, with
Brother, with refreshments for the wounded soldiers, & didn't I
recollect an officer coming out & speaking a little while with me
& giving me a bouquet before leaving." I did remember; he said,
'twas Gen. H. who told him about it afterwards.

I found six dear loving letters awaiting me, from my own
love, the idea of getting these was what made me shorten my visit
in Augusta.

Jan. 28th, 1866

Went to Aiken Thursday morning, spent the day with Lizzie,
went to the club party with them all. I enjoyed it unusually,
danced every dance, and went home where Nena Glover kept me
awake repeating poetry, nearly all night.

Spent Friday at Meta's. Lizzie is hypocriting, she has told
several *real* falsehoods to my prejudice to strangers, yet always
seems to be my dear friend, I do not intend going to stay with her
again, will return her hospitality and end it all, for *now*, I am
indifferent to her, wd. call her to account for what she has spread
about, but who told me of her stories, viz. Nellie, Meta & Nena G.
exacted a promise before informing me, that I should take no
notice nor compromise them as no one wants her enmity on account
of her tongue, *these* girls really like me, and believing me to be
neither, "deceitful nor dishonorable" as kindly imputed by her,

---

3. Paul Hamilton Hayne (1830–1886), romantic poet, literary editor and critic,
was born into a prominent, wealthy family in Charleston. His uncle was Robert Young Hayne, noted for his Senate debate with Daniel Webster in 1830
regarding states' rights and nullification. In the post–Civil War years Paul
Hayne became the representative poet of the South, and is considered an
important literary link between the Old South and the New South. In 1866 he
was living at his modest home, Copse Hill, 16 miles west of Augusta. Jay B.
Hubbell, *The South in American Literature, 1607–1900, 1954*, pp. 743–57.
4. Gen. John Bell Hood succeeded Gen. Joseph E. Johnston in command of the
Army of Tennessee on July 17, 1864. The failure of his offensive strategy
resulted in the decisive defeat of the Army of Tennessee in December 1864.
Hood was relieved of command upon his own request, January 23, 1865.

asked me *openly & honorably* about it. Now I'm very fond of Mrs. Coffin, always have been, & Charles & Amo, & in fact am intimate with the whole funeral procession, and am sorry of this nonsense of Lizzie's, I scorn anything underhand & low, this is both, & my contempt is honest. I won't bother Guerard with this now, this journal, he shall some day see, and that's enough.

On the train, I was handed a note from Roland Steiner, who is very sick & cannot come down as proposed, begs to be allowed to send me some choice reading next week, & says as soon as he is able will come down to discuss it.

I received a number of letters from my future lord, he is so kind & attentive & like mine, his tenderness & love seem to increase with every letter. I thank God for blessing me with such a great & noble love, it makes life sweet & precious.

Nena G. & George Croft[5] dined with me yesterday, Mary & Harry Coffin, Julia & John DeLettre with Mannie & Doolie, we had consequently enough for a pleasant dance.

Feb. 12th, 1866

Mannie & I went to the fancy ball, she as a flower girl, I as a white veiled nun, both had a magnificent time.

I remained four days with Meta, Tom was at home and helped make my time very pleasant. I think we are excellent friends quite fond of each other. He sat up one night 'till twelve, wrote me a long letter, called Meta out to take it to me, but changed his mind and wouldn't send it into me, so I don't know what he wrote about, as neither would tell me. He & Amo came around one morning about 8 o'cl. & stayed 'till 1, which time I spent in giving them a dancing lesson, then the Dr. came & we all went with him to drink lager beer. I returned on the train, Amo & Tom came as far as Johnstons. Tom begged me, when he moved up here to polish him, and to lend him my favorite books, &c., to read, says the army has made him rough and he wants the assistance of the

---

5. George William Croft, a native of Newberry County, S.C., was studying law at the University of Virginia. In 1870 he moved to Aiken where he opened a law practice and entered politics. *Cyclopedia of Eminent and Representative Men of the Carolinas in the Nineteenth Century, I, 1892,* pp. 195–96.

two most refined ladies he knows, Sallie Aldrich & myself. Ain't he complimentary?

Feb. 18th, 1866

Oh! he has come & gone, my own true love, and I love him more than I ever knew I could, he is so tenderly fond of me, I hardly feel worthy of him, but if love & devotion will make him happy, God knows he will be. He came at night, all were asleep but I & I was up writing to him, heard him come up the stairs, asked, "Who's there?" "Guerard," then I flew to Fa. to open the door, dressed & came down to him. I can't spare *one* of his precious words, even for here, I treasure them so much. But now he's gone & I feel as tho I had been dreaming all these two days, but such a happy almost *crazily* happy dream, God bless my own precious Guerard.

March 27th, 1866

I have just returned from spending a week with Mrs. Heyward. I went to see Meta & while there, Mr. Porcher a poor sick gentleman, who was there for his health, died suddenly, he asked me to play on the piano for him, & whenever I wd. stop, beg me to go on, & at last he got up & took both my hands & told me that I played just to suit him, & it was the first music he enjoyed for two years, he went to his room then & called his wife & told her she must go again to me & thank me for the enjoyment afforded him & while yet speaking to her he was seized by his death struggle, & died in a short while. Amo & the Dr. came 'round. Mrs. H. & Meta were both very sick & I was glad to be there to save them from some of the watch & sad preparations for the departure of poor Mrs. P. & her charge. Amo assisted a great deal too. Meta & Tom went down with them and I remained with Mrs. H. until Tom's return, he came last night & I came home this evening. Tom told me a good deal about my darling Guerard, everybody went to church this morning except him & I, and we talked the whole time, & I think, know & admire each other more than ever before, he begged me to call him Tom, and said there were but three people in the world he enjoyed conversing with, Amo, Mr. Geo. Heyward & my humble self, & says he often wishes I were a man, I'm afraid he & Guerard do not like each other very much, tho he speaks highly of him, I should be sorry if this is so; for I feel towards Tom as a sister & will always value his friendship & confidence. Mrs. H. told me she could not forgive Guerard for getting the start of Tom, last summer. I had to laugh, she didn't seem to think there was any difficulty, otherwise, not knowing, good lady, that my darling had every scrap of my heart in his—vest pocket. Well! well! I'm so happy.

April 3d, 1866

I spent five days in Augusta, with *the* girls, very pleasantly, I went to go to church & for my Easter communion, this I offered up for my dearest Guerard, God bless him & prosper him, Oh! I love him more & more every day, he is *so* kind & generous, do you know Journal, I let *four* weeks go by without writing to him, one line. I did it just to see what he'd do, well he kept on writing the whole time, & altho he begged me constantly to write, said he did not blame me a scrap, that he knew there was some good reason for my silence, but his continual disappointments were hard to bear, *my* letters being his only pleasures, & the only things that interrupt the monotony of his busy life, he is out all day working hard & for me too he says, and is *all alone* in the dreary country. I declare he is too kind & good & generous to me for my bad conduct, when I read his loving, sweet words today, I felt so provoked with myself that I had to come to my room & actually cry. I did; then sat up 'till two o'cl. to write him, my own darling Guerard.

Chapter Eleven

Marriage in the Offing: Wedding Preparations for November 6, 1866

April 14th, 1866

You know I positively forbid Maj. Buford to write to me any more & "quenched his ardour;" today I received a newspaper with his compliments, with a very affecting piece marked in it, I imagine he wrote it, it is his style.

Tom Heyward sent to ask me to allow him to escort me to the club party on the 12th, & Mrs. H. wrote to ask me to stay with her, so I went and had a delightful evening, Miss Maggie McD. who is staying with us, arranged my hair most beautifully, & I never had more compliments paid me. Dr. Coffin really quite overwhelmed me, I forgot to tell you how thick the Dr. & I are now, I never really knew him before this winter and we are the best of friends & always flirt like fun, when we meet, Oh! I have just had *such* a precious letter from Guerard, I most cried, because it had an end to it, will my love never have a limit? He begins now in his letters to say a great deal about October, when he wants me to be his wife. Now, this makes me so thoughtful, old Journal, I love Guerard better than the whole world beside, & would be utterly miserable if for an instant deprived of his precious love, it's my sunshine & my joy, & I know I can't help being *entirely* happy when I'll be with him forever & bear his name, and yet, you know, I don't want to be married I am, Oh! *so* happy *now*. I wish I could stay so for a *long, long* while, much longer than October, yet he wishes it *so* much, and is working *so* hard for me too, that I don't know how to manage, how can I possibly put him off. I hope something will happen to postpone it longer, for I am *so* happy & *so* selfish.

April 16th, 1866

Mrs. Wm. Gregg, the two Percivals & Lydia Croft,[1] spent the day with us, a day or two ago. Meta, Mannie & I went out to the Crofts to return Lydia's visit & spent the day with her very pleasantly. George [Croft] & I have struck up quite a friendship this winter. I always forget to mention him & my other desperate admirer. Nena Glover, I don't know which of the two express most enthusiastic love & admiration, but I see & hear quite enough of them to drop them here.

Mrs. Wm. Gregg invited me to go & spend the day with her, so I went, she had four or five of my friends to meet me & we had a nice day, & every sort of extravagant dainty to feast upon.

Amo & the Dr. sent me some delightful French novels & I'm lost in them.

[April] 30th, 1866

Grandmother came home on the 28th, as usual laden with beautiful presents for us all, she received her money from France amounting to $1,000, & gave the whole to Fa.,[2] my own noble, precious Fa. who is working, working, morn, noon & night to support us in comfort & to try to recover some of the essentials which the war raid stript us of, & what did *he* do with the money, which was wholly necessary to defray his expenses, pay debts & help to set him up in the life of *hard, hard* work, which at his advanced age & not strong health he is commencing. Why he divided it & sealed up $500.00 & gave it to me for my wedding outfit, kissing me, Oh, so tenderly & saying how grateful he was to God for sending it to me, & wishing he had thousands for his dear child. He sent Mother to Augusta with some of the rest & had us all fitted out so sweetly for spring & summer, & goes on

1. Mrs. William G. Gregg of Edgefield County, South Carolina, was the mother of Pauline's friend Rosa Clara Gregg Chafee. The two Percivals refers to the wife and daughter of Dr. W. F. Percival of Aiken. Lydia Croft was the sister of George William Croft.
2. During the difficult postwar years the DeCaradeuc family was aided by funds obtained from the French government as compensation for the emancipation in 1792 of the San Domingo slaves of Pauline's great-grandfather, Gen. Jean Baptiste DeCaradeuc.

working ten miles from us, dinnerless, & so cheerful & so good, *no one* knows what a heart my darling Fa. has, what unlimited & silent charity fills it, if ever an upright noble man existed it is he.

On the 26th, the day appropriated by the South for the decoration of the graves of her fallen sons, Mother, Fa., Mannie & I fixed up our little cemetery, Oh, *so* sweetly, with all the exquisite spring flowers & Fa. worked up all the beds so beautifully. In the afternoon, Mannie, Julia & I went to the graves of some poor soldiers near & decked them too with our trifling tributes of flowers.

I received today, a long letter from Robbie Gibbes, can't imagine what spirit has moved him to write to me, I can't possibly correspond with him, I have too many correspondents, who interest me more. My own dear Guerard sent me a sweet loving letter today too. He is coming to see me & I'm just ready to snap my head off for joy.

May 27th, 1866

Deary me, why haven't I written all these days, because I have too many blessings & joys to fill my heart I expect. Why, Guerard, God bless my own love, has been to see me again, & spent two short, short days with me, he came unexpectedly, I went to the cars to leave my dear Fa. there & to drive myself home, when to my joy & amazement Monsieur G. jumped off & drove me home. I believe I love him a thousand times better, he is good & noble & sweet & darling, my *own, own, own* Guerard, I felt in a dream the whole time, my spirits all went, & I just felt quiet & too happy to even think. My only trial is in having him *so* far off, if he were only where I could see him often, should be *entirely* happy. And he has been gone now nearly two weeks, again God bless him, & keep him safe, for he is my sunshine & my life.

I spent four or five days with Meta, Master Tom managed, as usual, to be at home most of the time, and was as entertaining & *quarrelsomely* agreeable as ever.

Lizzie Coffin spent all last week with me, she is too double face to suit me, one would think from her manner, she *loved* me, whilst the many unkind things she & friend Min. have circulated about Guerard & me proved the opposite but I promised myself not to think of this again, as I have forgiven & now mean to forget.

Mr. Redmond wrote to ask me to meet him & Mel on the train at Aiken to tell them good-bye ere they left for N.Y., which I did, both were very kind & *obliging* & pleasant.

I'm plaiting my darling a palmetto hat to keep the sun from his dear old head, & Mel carried a piece of my hair to have made into studs & sleeve buttons in N.Y. for him, I wish they were here already.

June 1st, 1866

Mannie and I went to the club party last night, Tom, of course, escorted us, I of course, danced every time & had a very pleasant evening, how much I wish my own love could take me to these parties, last summer, when he was at them, they were the first parties at Aiken that I could make up my mind to attend since Brother & Tonio used to take me, consequently they were very trying to me & I felt lonely & sad most of the time, but now I am more accustomed & have gradually crept back into my old stand at the Aiken parties in which position, Guerard never has seen me.

I declare Amo & I know each other, instinctively, *too well*, I can always tell what effect my words are going to have on him before I utter them, altho, to all appearances he is more phlegmatic than anyone I know, 'tis only put on, he *feels greatly*, but generally has as much self-command. Last night in coming from the refreshment room, for the first time since I began calling him, Mr., I forgot & called him Amo again, his hand seemed unconsciously to fall on mine in his arm, it was trembling like a leaf, I, as unconsciously & very calmly, withdrew my arm, making some commonplace remark, this, as I knew would, immediately bring back his coldness & calm, nor did he again offer his arm, tho we promanaded together for some time after, chatting as pleasantly as possible, he did not dance again with me, but came 'round to Tom Heyward's after the party, in the highest spirits, I played for them & we did not retire until after four o'clock. Now this is the strange influence he & I exert over each other, 'tho never in word have we mentioned it to any one, or to ourselves, it is an inate understanding, when one is excited the other's perfect calm immediately quiets the excitement, & his or her coldness calls the pride of the other.

When he gave me the particulars of George Lalane's death last year, if it had been anyone but Amo, I could not have concealed my emotion, but—his cold calmness about it—one of his bosom friends too—kept me perfectly cool, 'tho I *knew* how much he felt. Then the night of Mr. Porcher's death in Aiken, when only he & I were in the parlour, every agonizing shriek of the dying man seemed to pierce my heart, & I was becoming wretchedly excited, until his command & calmness summoned mine, he began repeating to me some verses in German; this seemed heartless, but altho I knew he felt almost as much as I did, it immediately gave me perfect command & steadiness to continue assisting *quietly*. Sometime he will talk with me on subjects that he knows are congenial for ever so long & be attentive & friendly, then again will avoid me with studied care, not even for a moment meet a glance. All these changes, I understand, & am *always* his cool, quiet, unnoticing friend. He never has mentioned Guerard to me once, and whenever I bring the conversation to anything concerning him, he immediately changes it. Sometimes he will fix his eyes on me & seem buried in thought, this don't even make me uncomfortable, altho when I look into his eyes, small as they are, I can read a great deal. But my friend, this is enough, I've known your secret for a long while & will keep it even as closely as you do. Thank God for Guerard's precious love, it is just what overflows my whole soul and keeps out every other thought & care. Sometimes, I fear that my love for him is too much like idolatry.

Oh dear me! I have offended or rather Meta says hurt, Master Tom's feelings, he gave me a beautiful pair of soft kid gauntlets the other day, & I wouldn't accept them at his house. Meta says he is very much hurt & says he don't see why I can't even accept a present from him. I couldn't pretend to, tho, I hate to get presents from my own people even.

July 2d, 1866

My dear Grandmother's illness kept me from writing all this time. She has been at death's door, and I thank God, was restored to us & is now almost well again.

Meta spent last night with me & begged me to go up on Friday & spend Saturday & Sunday with her, as Tom wd. be at home & is always so delighted to find me there. I'll do no such thing, let him find time to come here if he wants to see me.

I do not hear often from Guerard, he has few opportunities, he says, to go to the P.O. which is 15 miles off.

Mel sent my studs, *I* think them very pretty, wish now I could give them to my sweet love.

Cousin Maxine spent the last two weeks with us.

Guerard says he looks upon his marriage in Oct. as a fixed fact. I treat the subject with silence to him, for dear me, I don't think I can possibly make up my mind or—trousseau for yet awhile.

August 19th, 1866

Really I scarcely ever write here now, I'm either too busy, or too happy or something, for I never have time.

I paid two pleasant visits to Augusta, & spent one other week at the Parrott's & Meta's. Went to be Belle's bridesmaid & had a pleasant time at the wedding. Guerard met me in Augusta & came home with me, & spent a whole week with us, he was a thousand times dearer & sweeter than ever, sometimes I'm afraid I love that boy too much, I can't think or pray for anything else but him, . . . [illegible] & he,—is so devoted, so kind & noble in every way . . . [illegible].

Dr. Coffin saw my dear Mother today and says her spine is effected a good deal, that she must keep in bed for two weeks, but greatly relieved us by saying that her illness required nothing but care & had no dangerous symptoms at all, before that, I was wretchedly uneasy, now my heart is light again.

Oct. 30th, 1866

I cannot pretend to journalize the crowd of events that have transpired since last I wrote. At home now, there is but one absorbing topic & occupation, my approaching marriage & its preparations.

Mother, G. Mother, Tante & Mannie, give me their entire time, and we are all most busy sewing & planning. My own darling parents, spare themselves in *no wise* in trying to have everything as nice as possible for me, and straightened & embarrassed as my fond Father is, he has given & expended for & on me to his very last cent, refusing to get even one new article for himself, that I might not be without even trifles, & Mother is just the same, more devoted, loving, unselfish & self-abnegating parents never lived . . . [illegible]. I feel that I never, never, can love & cherish them sufficiently to return their utter devotion to me, but all this is in my heart and I didn't mean to put it here.

"My Boy" paid me two visits since August, each one leaving my heart more entirely his than ever before; he is of the truest, purest metal, & will stand among thousands, the more I know him the more I discover to love and respect; and his boundless love & devotion are treasures, for which my heart is filled with gratitude to God.

We are to be married on 6th November, it is very near now, yet altho I'm a little bit nervous at times, I'm not scared at all, my heart is too filled with love to admit any fears.

I have received some very beautiful letters from my friends, which I prize greatly, and some very pretty presents from them too.

One dreadful thing has happened, an elegant brocade silk which Mother gave me for my handsomest dress, came home from the dressmaker in Augusta, utterly ruined, so scantly cut that it won't fit over my hoop. I was most frantic.

Aunt Mary [della Torre] has chosen my bridal dress in Baltimore for me, I asked her to do so on account of her exquisite taste, she writes, it is of white silk, with tulle veil reaching over the train, which is a yard & a half long.

Mary Gregg was married in Sept. I went to the wedding and the party afterwards, & enjoyed both evenings intensely. There I met Dr. Sterling Eve of Augusta, who has been sending me messages for eighteen months, in fact, we all but knew each other, & our families have been friends from time immemorial, he is strikingly handsome and very elegant in manner, &c. he directed all his attentions to my humble self, whom he calls his old friend, & I found him very pleasant.

I went to Augusta & after he heard I was expected, met me at the depot in his buggy, & was otherwise quite devoted, tries very hard to convince me that Guerard is not *"the one,"* &c., &c., all fun, of course.

I went again to Augusta last week & staid two days to have my dresses finished, &c. He called both mornings, took me to drive in a charming buggy & spendid black horse, and spent both evenings with me too, trying to be more & more fascinating each time; but, ha! ha! he found *no place* left, even on the surface, to take hold of, and had e'en to acknowledge himself completely outgeneraled; in spite of the remarkable beauty & fascination, which I think his vanity believes irresistible.

I have had *so* many visits from my friends lately, that it interferes greatly with my work, they say they want to see me as much now, as they can, as I'm soon to leave.

Sometimes I feel, Oh! so sad about leaving my sweet home & beloved parents. I am & always have been so dearly attached to home & so easily made homesick, I never could stand to be absent more than one month at farthest & now I don't know what I shall do, if I did not know what a powerful love my own Guerard will have always for one who gives up everything nearest & dearest on earth, willingly & happily for his dear sake. I do not think I will write here again, dear old Journal & subscribe myself now for the last time perhaps, with emotions of great joy & sadness.

Pour le dernier temps—PAULINE DE CARADEUC!

1867

Chapter Twelve

Married Life in Bluffton: Hard Work, Happiness, and Grief

March 13th, 1867

I thought that I had taken leave of you dear old Journal, when I had signed for the last time my name at the end of the last page, but I find you have been too good a friend for me to relinquish and I have added these pages to tell you a little of my married life.

I think I will go all the way back to Nov. 6th, 1866, the day of my wedding. Bishop Lynch[1] performed the ceremony which took place at 9 P.M. He (the Bishop) arrived at 8 o'cl., & when I had finished dressing & my veil was on, I went to him in the room joining my own, and from him received absolution, ere taking so important a step in life; he then went down to the parlour, & my dear Father came for me, and at the foot of the steps, put my arm in my Guerard's, he and Mother followed us into the parlour, where our eighteen attendants were standing in a circle 'round the Bishop; soon it was over, and our new life was opened to us.

The wedding was a very gay one, all of our young friends were present; the band played joyfully and the dancing, laughing & merry making was kept up with great glee until supper at twelve. The table was beautiful & delightful, all seemed happy & gay, and there was none of the usual wedding stiffness, but in all that crowd, I saw but one form, felt but one presence,—my husband's—I was in a dream.

The attendants all remained the next day & next night too, we remained three days at home, then left for Charleston, where we had a reception of Guerard's relatives in the City. And then we

---

1. Patrick N. Lynch became the third Bishop of Charleston in 1858.

came here to Bluffton,[2] where I was received by My Boy's kind parents & immediate family, most warmly and affectionately. We came immediately to our own little home. A sweet home indeed, so prettily & comfortably furnished; everything looking bright & new and nice servants, &c., all giving me proof of my darling's love and *great* thought.

And that love to which I cling so strongly, soon taught me to feel at home and happy, in his house; all was sunshine & joy in our lives, he was even more to me than I ever pictured he would be; but why do I say *"he was?"*, I mean he *is*. I was thinking of those uninterrupted days.

About two weeks after our marriage, Guerard's two cousins, Mary Strobhart & Harriet Gadsden came to pay him a visit, they were both strangers to me, and at first it was quite a trial to me, but I soon learned to know them, and then I did not mind. While they were here Little Bluffton crept out of its snail shell and three dances were gotten up, these must be recorded "for a precident."

The girls spent ten days with us, and soon after Meta Heyward came. I was delighted, for it seemed like a home face among so many utter strangers, & you know Journal, how easily homesick poor Polly gets.

And when sometimes my darling would be at the plantation a whole day, I would feel decidedly blue, and wish so much for some one from home, then when I would hear his footsteps, all "Mes Vapens noir," would fly away, and I would wonder why I felt dull. About a month after our marriage, my precious Father was taken desperately ill, all hope left them at home, & they sent for me. My darling took me immediately to him, and we found him out of danger. A merciful God had raised him up. We staid a week home to-gether, then My Boy returned to Bluffton on business, & I remained to join him in Charleston the following week.

Fa. went down with me, My darling met us at the depot, and I thought, when I saw him after so long an absence, that his face

———————

2. Bluffton, South Carolina (Beaufort District), was incorporated as a town in 1852. Originally settled in the early 1800s as a summer resort for rice planters and their families, the community was located on a high bluff on the May River. It was first called May River and Later Kirk's Bluff (for one of its leading families); in 1840 at a town meeting its name was changed to Bluffton. Caldwell, ed., *No II, A Longer Short History of Bluffton . . .*, 1988, p. 8.

never looked so precious before. The sadness of separation was truly compensated by the joy, the delight of again being to-gether.

Those were such happy days we spent in the City to-gether all unclouded; and we were so enraptured at being once again with each other after exchanging our first letters as husband & wife.

Fa. staid three days in town too, at the same house. We returned then to Bluffton after an absence of one month from our sweet new home.

I did not feel homesick again for a long while. My trip home & all my long talks with Mother helped me a great deal.

Housekeeping does not trouble me, in spite of the terrible times, and my inexperience, & the numberless complaints among housekeepers.

We have a plenty of trouble with servants, that is, annoyance, but in the scale of life these are minor weights.

Our days passed quietly and as counterparts all along. My darling being at the plantation[3] almost every day and often at nights too, where he is going ahead with wonderful energy, if any one is deserving of success, My Boy is, for he is untiring in his exertions, and the unusual amount of care and trouble which altho so young a man, have accumulated upon him, he stands bravely & does not spare himself one iota.

And now it comes for me to record here the great sorrow that God has sent to him, & to his family. His dear & honored father, Mr. George Heyward, was cruelly murdered on the public road, on the 1st of March 1867.[4] 'Twas a frightful blow to his large family who held him in such love & veneration, and indeed he

---

3. Buckingham Plantation, located just west of Hilton Head Island, near Bluffton, in Beaufort District.
4. On the morning of March 1, 1867, George Cuthbert Heyward went to visit Buckingham Plantation which he and his sons were cultivating. When he failed to come home to Bluffton at the usual dinner hour, his family became uneasy. Soon thereafter his riderless horse returned home, and his sons and a few neighbors set out immediately to search for him. His body was found at 8 o'clock that night, lying in a ditch close to the road with a rifle ball through his forehead. At the time it was believed that he was murdered by a negro in his employ. According to family lore, however, an old soldier on his deathbed in Alabama many years later confessed to the killing as an act of revenge because of a reprimand given him by Capt Heyward during the war. *Charleston Daily Courier*, Mar. 8, 1867; *Savannah Daily News and Herald*, Mar. 4, 1867.

was a noble & righteous man, one to whom Shakespeare's well
known words would justly apply, "He was a man, take him all in
all we shall not look upon his like again." Of the woe & affliction
that his cruel death has brought to his family, I cannot write; to
witness & share my husband's sorrow is a sad, sad appointment
from our Lord, and my prayer is, that He will bless & strengthen
me, that I may be truly a comfort, a consolation & even a blessing
to my husband, in these days of sorrow, and grave, serious care.

March 14th, 1867

I find myself writing here again, for I am lonely this morning,
and you are a faithful companion, old Journal, with whom I can
communicate, and altho you cannot answer or speak to me save
thro the lapse of years, I find you a comfort.

Loulie[5] slept with me last night, My dear lord having gone to
Charleston, day before yesterday, he will be away four days more.
The mornings I find go quickly enough, for I have plenty of
occupations, but in the evenings I grow tired of the house & of
myself, so I spend them over at the other house, where my husband's family always give me an affectionate welcome, indeed I
am dependent on their charity entirely for companionship, for my
acquaintance in the village is limited. A few persons called when
I first came, but a concatenation of circumstances prevented my
returning their calls, for so long a time as to give the semblance of
indifferentism, consequently I am still an entire stranger even to
my nearest neighbors, but you know, Polly is not dependent on
society for comfort & content, altho I have always enjoyed it.

This is a dark & dismal day, pouring rain & very cold. Old
Peter brought me some wood and made a nice fire for me, before
which I have been sitting ever since Lou left this morning. I
walked to the window in hope of seeing some of the dismal things
Washington Irving clothes with such poetic interest in his "rainy
days," Mais helos! I could not view things with his happy eyes, so
I have returned to my fire as being the more attractive. Where
like the old Frau Matha, I hear the unrelenting patter on the

5. Probably a reference to Guerard Heyward's young cousin Ella Louisa Heyward,
   age 12, daughter of Mr. and Mrs. Thomas Savage Heyward.

house tops, and now it is, sundown, that it would be so if there were any sun to go down, and as I am still sitting here in my rocking chair, and waiting for Lou and Dan,[6] who will come again, after tea to sleep here.

Sunday, March 16th, 1867

How I long for tomorrow to come & bring My Boy to me, it seems as tho' he has been away a month & I have yet to wait 30 hours. I'm lonely without him, I feel like a different being when he is with me; to-day it is light again after three days of dismal rain.

Perhaps my darling Mother will come too, to-morrow. Would that I had more patience in waiting for them, I am too eager for my own good.

March 19th, 1867

The two past, have been the happiest days I have spent for a long, long while. My dear boy, spent them with me, and it is so rare that I see more than just a little of him, that I am truly happy when I do, he took me to drive thro the pretty woods, & I go out so seldom now, that it was a treat to ride along thro the cool air, then to have him with me, made my heart so light, & made everything look prettier.

To-day he is at New River again,[7] and will return in two days; they will be blank, 'till the dawn of the third.

March 28th, 1867

I have been sick in bed all day, & alone in the house, even our servant was out all day. Lou came a few minutes this morning &

---

6. Dan is probably Guerard Heyward's young brother Thomas Daniel Heyward, age 15.
7. A reference to the rice plantation of Guerard's father located on the New River near Hardeville, South Carolina. According to the Federal Census of 1860, George Cuthbert Heyward of "The Bluff," St. Peter's Parish, Beaufort District, owned 100 or more slaves.

promised to come to-night to sleep with me. Guerard left me at daylight to be away two days. The family are busy, moving to another house, a large one. Would that it were not large enough to accomodate us, for, Oh, Journal, just think of it, in three day's time we are to move & to live with Guerard's enormous family, the thought is alarming, and [illegible].

The Interim Years

1868-1874

The Interim Years

Following the tragic death of his father Guerard, the eldest of twelve surviving offspring, became the head of the large Heyward family. His eleven siblings ranged in age from twenty-two years to one year. Guerard, although only twenty-three years old himself, took on the responsibility of helping his widowed mother support the family. He soon discovered that planting was not an agreeable occupation and afforded a less than adequate economic base for such an enterprise.

Guerard moved to Savannah in 1868 and took a job as bookkeeper with Bates & Comer, cotton factors. He obtained a room at the Pulaski House, where he lived until he could move his family to Savannah. In the meantime Pauline returned to Montmorenci to await the birth of their first child, Elise, who was born on May 9, 1868

Pauline's father, Achille DeCaradeuc, also abandoned his efforts to support his family by planting cotton at Montmorenci. He became chief engineer and land agent with the South Carolina Railroad and in 1869 returned to Charleston, where he rented a house at No. 6 Aiken Row. It was here that Pauline gave birth, December 3, 1869, to twins, Rose and Pauline, who died three months later.

Achille DeCaradeuc sold Montmorenci on February 28, 1870, to Augustus A. Ruxton for the sum of $10,000.[1] Six months later Pauline's grandmother, Maxime DeCaradeuc, died at the age of eighty-one in Charleston.

On June 1, 1871, Pauline's fourth daughter, Margaret (Maude), was born at the DeCaradeuc home in Charleston. She was named for Pauline's only sister, Mannie, who had died three months before. Three years later Guerard and Pauline had their fifth daughter and named her Pauline (Nina).

A few years after establishing himself in business in Savannah, Guerard moved his mother and younger siblings to a home

---

1. Copy of Bill of Sale, courtesy of Mary DeCaradeuc Bartholomew.

at the Isle of Hope near Savannah, and assisted the older boys in finding employment in Savannah. George Cuthbert obtained a job as a warehouse clerk with J. L. Villalonga Company, and Thomas Daniel (Dan) became a clerk and later a bookkeeper with H. M. Comer & Company. A few years later William Marion became a clerk in the United States Court clerk's office; Thomas Savage obtained employment as a clerk with Seigfried & Co.; and John Alexander became a clerk with Branch & Cooper Co.[2]

By 1874 Pauline and Guerard, their three daughters, and Guerard's brothers George and Dan were living in a home on Abercorn Street in Savannah. It was here that Pauline once again took up her journal to record her thoughts and feelings about the important events in her life.

2. The United States Census for 1870, Beaufort County, South Carolina, shows Guerard's mother, Elizabeth Heyward, still living in Bluffton with Elizabeth, age 10; John, 8; Caroline, 6; and Nathaniel, 4. James Cuthbert, age 25, had remained in Bluffton to farm.

The Journal of
Pauline
DeCaradeuc Heyward

1875-1888

Chapter Thirteen

Motherhood:
Elise, Maude, and Nina

Records

Little book you have a part to play
In the sweet drama of childhood's May,
Your snowy leaves I now design
As records of three daughters mine.
Three babes they are of promise rare,
Three gladsome hearts, three faces fair.
Herein I'll mark their early bents,
Their childhood's years, their life's events,
I see midst visions far away
Two forms bent low, two heads turned grey,
This little book between them lies,
Records of their life's sunrise;
A bridge of flowers refreshed by tears
Which all must drop to fleeting years,
A bridge which links them firm & fast,
Unto those years—the happy past!
A Father & Mother bending low
Hear music from their "long ago."

March 14th, 1875

At the time of commencing to record a few of the events in the lives of my little girls, I think it appropriate to give their ages, and a short account of each.

To begin then with Elise, our first born. She was born on 9th May, 1868, at Montmorenci, S. C.

I have often called her my rosebud, for this reason—viz: about three weeks before her birth, I was walking in the garden at my old home, Montmorenci, the roses were in the perfection of their glory, we gathered them by *the bushel* of the most exquisite & rare varieties. My enjoyment of them was intense, as I had no flowers for months. As I walked from bush to bush, I was particularly charmed by one "La Reine," which seemed really to have more roses than leaves. I noticed upon it one tiny rosebud hidden away under the leaves. Now, thought I, this bud shall be my omen, the day that it blooms, may Heaven send me a little rosebud daughter. And to mark it, I took a blue ribbon from my hair & tied around it.

Three weeks after, my Elise came to me, and I told her dear father about my rosebud, he went & returned bringing me an exquisite rose just blown, with the ribbon still tied to the stem!

Mademoiselle Elise conducted herself very creditably after the fashion of babies, and at five months her *first tooth* appeared. She got out her teeth with great ease, and had no serious sickness, altho several minor attacks of indisposition, which always alarmed us mortally. She *walked at fourteen months*, being too fat to carry her weight earlier. Elise began school at the age of five in 1873.

In the summer of '74, she was very sick with fever, & to break it, we confided her to the loving care of Aunt Rose, who took her to New York, where she got quite well & spent several weeks, then they finished the summer at Brookland, near Baltimore,[1] here my poor darling was most severely bitten by a dog. It has given her a terror of those animals, which I fear she will never overcome. She is blessed with health, having never had any disease, save the mumps when three years old. She is now six years old & is considered a very handsome child. Her disposition is lovely, being all tenderness & gentleness, she is easily managed. A few serious words, is the only reproof she ever needs, she has truly a *merry* heart & where ever she is there is sure to be lots of fun & laughter, consequently she is a great favorite with her little friends & is always in demand amongst them.

But I shall write of her character & dispositon as they develop & note them by her own words & actions.

My little twin daughters, Pauline & Rose, were born in Charleston, 3rd Dec. 1869. They were exquisitely, lovely, delicately, frail little darlings, it was only by untiring care & devotion,

---

1. The family home of Mary Gordon Norris, widow of Pauline's uncle Peter della Torre.

that they lived three months, they died in March, Pauline on 9th & Rose on 10th. In death they are not divided.

My little Elise had to begin her office as comforter to me when we lost them, she herself being but 22 months old.

Margaret, our fourth daughter, was born in Charleston (No. 6 Aiken's Row, 5th house from Meeting St.) June 1st, 1871. She was sent, my dear Mother said, as a comfort & blessing to us all, three months after the death of my beloved & only sister, whose name she bears. We call her Maude, because once, while chatting with that same sweet sister, I said, "If ever I have another daughter, I will call her Margaret for you." She replied, "If you do, please call her Maude 'for short', I think it so sweet a name." And so I have done as she wished & my little Margaret is called Maude, almost entirely.

She was a magnificent specimen of an infant, but very nervous, her *first tooth* appeared, when five months old, she cut the others with great trouble, and the second summer of her life, we almost lost her from convulsions, she had hot fevers with every tooth, and yet strange to say they never pulled her down, she *ever* has been the picture of a splendidly developed child, *noble* in her appearance and also in her character. She has a strong will and a most unusual amount of presence of mind, as an instance of the last, when she was not quite three years old, she was playing in the yard with several little girls older than herself, they were playing on a large wooden box which fell over on a kitten, the unfortunate little animal screamed with all the agony of a broken back, the children all ran up the yard steps in terror, calling for me to rescue it, when fat little Maude with her forehead all puckered up with heartfelt concern, ran & lifted the heavy box & pulled out the poor little kitty, and had it in her arms ere I could reach the yard.

Many other circumstances have occurred, which show her to possess a great deal of character, and as her heart is of the very warmest and most loving & her disposition sweet, I think she will make a fine woman. She is brim full of mischief, and only the other day, I knew by her extreme quiet she was after something forbidden. I called to her, "Maude what are you doing?", she lisped out to be sure, "I'se in mischiefs," and upon my following my words to see what she was after, I found her seated on the pantry floor with the sugar dish in her lap, enjoying herself to the fullest extent.

The young lady can be reasoned and coaxed into doing anything, but if I try to *coerce* her against her will, it is needless to
attempt it, I have tried by threats, locking up, whipping & finally
putting to bed, (which series of punishments, lasted from after
dinner to tea time) to get her to say "thank you," she had determined *not* to say it, and she did not either, altho she cried until
she broke out in purple spots, over the punishments, I have avoided
another such scene by managing her entirely thro her heart. And
her love for me is so great & sweet, that a few words can generally
subdue her. Maude is now four years old, her skin is lily white,
pure blond, her eyes are soft brown & her almost flaxen curls
nearly reach her waist, her form is beautiful & she is as plump as
a rice bird.

She has the unfortunate habit of sucking her thumb, which I
in vain try to break her of. She has only been away from me once,
when she went to Charleston with her Grandpa to visit Grand-
mama, she loves them devotedly, and spent two weeks most happily there.

Elise is a little darker than Maude, being a light brunette,
with bright brown eyes, & soft brown hair, her face is round &
rosy, and she too is very plump, her hands are beautiful.

Pauline [Nina], our baby is now—*AUGUST, 1875.*—seventeen
months old. We call her the beauty of the family, as she has
beautiful auburn hair, very fair skin, large brown eyes & the
longest black eye lashes I ever saw, she is slightly formed, & very
graceful in her movements. She is the best baby we have ever
had, I have not lost an hour's rest with her since her birth, and
she is a winsome wee thing all day long. *She walked* at twelve
months, cut her first tooth at five, and with a few trifling attacks
of fever, she has out all her hard ones now. We brought her to the
Isle of Hope,[2] where we are spending the summer, in order that
she may be strengthened by the salt water, in her teething.

---

2. The Isle of Hope is located on the Skidaway River in Chatham County, near
   Savannah. Guerard had moved his mother and younger brothers and sisters
   there soon after establishing himself in business in Savannah.

May 1876

We returned to Savannah[3] in November, after spending a summer free of care & full of happiness, our children grew in strength,
grace & beauty, and with the blessing of health, and affectionate
intercourse with my husband's beloved mother & family, we were
as happy as ever in our lives.

My Elise went to Charleston to school. Her dear Grandpapa
came for her & they left me at the end of October, her amount of
education consisting in the knowledge of her A.B.C. and spelling
in two syllables. Maude & I missed her very much and we both
had several cries, for "Sister" when she went.

Immediately after our return to the City, we were called
upon to bear one of life's saddest trials, Guerard's dear mother
was stricken down in her health & strength, and after a brief
illness passed away into her Heavenly rest.[4] I loved her scarcely
less than did my husband, and sorrow over her loss, as—after my
own parents—my dearest & best friend. It shall be my sacred care
to keep her memory fresh & beloved by our little ones, whom she
tenderly loved. Nor can I omit this opportunity of telling them, in
a few words, of her beautiful character. She was as near perfection as any one could be, combining the beauties of mind & body
& character, so powerfully in its *sweetness* & nobility, that her
influence was of the happiest & strongest sort over all who were
associated with her. To know her slightly was to love her & to
know her intimately, was to love & reverence.

I carried my two little ones over to Charleston to spend the
Christmastide, with my dear Father & Mother, & after a month
of sweet quiet with them, we returned home, parting again with
that "apple of my eye" Elise, she had improved so nicely at school,
and was so lovely & sweet. Nothing but a knowledge of the good
to *her* & comfort to my parents, reconciled me to the prolonged
separation.

We moved into our own sweet new home in Jan. 1876 (New
Houston St.). My sweet child Maude has been my inseparable
companion all winter, I never went out without her, and her very

---

3. By this time Pauline and Guerard had moved their family into a new home on
   New Houston Street.
4. According to the Death Record, Elizabeth Martha Guerard Heyward died of
   "inflamation of the brain," on November 12, 1875, at the age of fifty-one.

intelligent & unceasing prattle has beguiled me of care or sad thoughts. Nina too, the little toad! is a perfect little chatterbox, she is two years old, & calls us Father & Mother of her own accord; it is too sweet from her rosy little lips; she is very lovely; 'tho many persons consider Maude the prettiest. I am very proud of my little chicks, for besides their beauty they have such golden promises in their hearts each character is a study & each child requires her own peculiar management, this it is the business of *my* life to develop, may I be equal to the task!

Elise returned from Charleston in April 1876, her dear Grandmamma brought her, and our joy at once more having our bright & precious Birdie, is great indeed! She learned rapidly at school & my greedy ears drink in the sound of her sweet little voice as she reads over her lessons to me daily. She goes to school to Madame Chastanet,[5] opposite to us & has begun to learn French.

I teach my lady Maude every day, just a little, & she now knows her letters & spells in three letters, aged 4! While little Nina is made radiantly happy with a rag doll, which she rolls up & down in the piazza in her little carriage.

---

5. The wife of Frederick Chastanet, French Vice-Consul, who lived on New Houston Street. *Haddock's Savannah, Ga. Directory, General Advertiser*, compiled by T. M. Haddock (Savannah: J. H. Estill, 1871), p. 94.

Chapter Fourteen

A Happy Event:
The Birth of
Jacob Guerard Heyward, Jr.

Toccoa, Ga.,[1] Oct., 1876

This past summer has been a very eventful one in the Guerard Heyward family! On the 9th of August, Master J. G. Heyward arrived. Lovingly welcomed by his Father, Mother & Grandmother, and clamorously welcomed by his three pretty sisters, who all stood 'round him, with noses out of joint, gazing with wonder at his calm little face. He weighed 10 pounds at his birth and persons said was a very handsome baby. My love for this perfect boy is pure rapture, The words, "My son" have a magic sound to me. He looks like his dear Father, bears his honored name and will, I trust be like him in all his chivalric nature. Just three weeks after our son's birth, the yellow fever broke out in Savannah; virulent & fatal, from the first;[2] our Dr. said, if we would save our children, we must leave the City, and this caused me the saddest parting from their beloved Father.

It was imperative that he should remain where his business is, and for me to leave him in danger was a trial almost too great, and yet, should I lose our precious children? It ended by his sending us to Gainesville,[3] where we spent six weeks. The fever raged with a violence unequaled before, it amounted to a plague, and

1. Toccoa, a mountain resort located in Habersham County, is 93 miles N.E. of Atlanta.
2. Figures appearing in the Savannah *Morning News* November 28, 1876, taken from "Mortuary Record of Savannah During the Epidemic of 1876," list total deaths during August through November of that year as 1,574, of which 940 were from yellow fever. Georgia Collection, GHS: Georgia Pamphlets, v. 6.
3. Gainesville, capital of Hall County, Georgia, 53 miles N.E. of Atlanta, was a popular summer resort and health spa with mineral springs.

129

tortured by constant fear & anxiety for my husband's safety, I have been more miserably unhappy than ever in my life before.

We left Savannah on Sept. 1st, and 'tis now 18th of Oct. and the fever still seizes every new victim with unabating fury. My girls share my anxiety and comfort me with their sweet childish sympathy. When I read to them their father's letter each night, with the blessed assurance of his continued health they both say so fervently, "Thank God" & it touches my very heart to hear their earnest little voices praying for him; even our little two-year-old Nina, says, on her knees, "Pray Dod bless my Papa & keep him tite well, dare not dat's enough prayers." Maude was very thoughtful one night, she came to me and said, "Mama, I want to go to Savannah and take the yellow fever & let my Papa come away." She had an idea that a sacrifice could be made to save her father and she, with her own beautiful characteristic unselfishness, was ready to make it. Maude gets into all the scraps of the family, does more mischief than any, yet she has grand qualities, & a very beautiful heart. She went with me into a lady's room a few nights ago, and was given two sugar plums, when we came out, she said, "Mama those sugar plums were so delightful, I just tasted a little piece of one, and then shut my hands tight, so I couldn't eat them, and I kept one for Sister & one for Nina." And sure enough she gave her sister one, and Nina being asleep in her bed, she put up in her drawer, the other, with the little piece bitten off, and soon the next morning she gave it to Nina; and Maude loves candy better than anything else!

My three girls excite great admiration, Elise is a perfect little lady, and so pretty too, I have been complimented on her repeatedly, and Nina is a peculiarly beautiful child, she has very odd little ways of her own. They all three have exquisite skins, and were considered the beauties among the many children at the Piedmont Hotel at Gainesville.

Our son has grown splendidly, he weighs now, 18 lbs. and is not yet three months. I long so for his father's acquaintance, he was so young—just three weeks old—when he had to run for his life; he is simply magnificent in his form & appearance, & *very good at night*, which is the very best quality in a young man of his age.

July, 1877

My boy Guerard does not teeth as young as any of his sisters, his first tooth did not appear until he was 9 months old, & now at eleven months, he has but five out. However he is the finest of all the babes, his limbs are elegant, large strong & elegantly formed, his chest is a perfect model, so broad & thick, he will make a powerful man if he fulfills his early promise. He now *walks* all about, at *eleven months*, as strongly as a two-year-old boy, & he calls, Papa, Mama, Bow-bow, &c. and understands every word that is said to him. I have never seen a more intelligent baby, or one possessed of so much mirth & good nature, he smiles & jabbers to every eye that he catches, he does not seem to be aware that he is a teether, for he is enormously fat & very hearty, he enjoys his plate of okra soup as tho he were an old epicure, & when hungry, points to the safe & says, "Tata."

Letter from Jack to Papa

I sink it is time, my darlin' old Dad
Dat 'oo dot a letter from you own 'ittle lad,
I'm grow'd a big boy, and gettin' dood too,
Dat's fine for six weeks, I sink so—don't 'oo?
It's true that I fusses most all of the day,
But then with us Babies, that's always the way.
And what is the use of fine lungs in a fellow
If he can't, when he wishes, take a good bellow.
The fact is the folks treat me very much bad,
They don't understand us, my darlin' ole Dad,
Sometimes, I wake up quite in for a frolic,
I'm teased—when I cry, they call that the colic.
Mama, she runs for the hot peppermint,
And nurse pours it down with a heart hard as flint,
When I open my eyes at this big world to peep,
They toss and they shake me, yite straight back to
    sleep.
And den when I yearly does have a big pain

"Oh, he's hungry," down the tea goes again.
And yet how I'm growin'! Mama calles me her joy,
She says I'm just like 'oo, I'm Papa's own boy.
I'se dot bright blue eyes, & a big double chin.
And a dear little mouth, for the pap to go in,
If I'm cross in the day, I am splendid at night,
I dozes 'ite thro 'till the sun rises bright.
And now Master Papa I sink I am done
You must yite a long answer to

Your own 'ittle, SON

We took our little family down to Tybee Island,[4] last month and spent a couple of weeks there, that we might with them, enjoy the surf bathing. It was delicious in the surf and the prettiest sight in the world, to see the little crowd, with their pretty plump limbs in the water, perfectly intoxicated with delight, Maude, as usual was the most venturesome, and once she escaped me, and I held my breath to see her saucy face marched up to an enormous wave, & see her spring up to it with glee, when I would have been in dread, she was knocked down, of course, but got up and was making for the next, when I captured her, and took her further out. Little Nina went in with her night gown on, for a bathing suit, and the little burnished head beauty, would walk into the water with delight, until it would reach her skirts, then she would hold it up high & higher as the water deepened, until finding it would get wet, she would cry & beg to be taken out as she didn't love to get her gown wet. Elise put on any number of airs, & I believe fancied herself a mermaid over & over, and even little Guerard was fearless & happy in the breakers. Then the walks on the broad beach & the picking up of beautiful shells, all combined to make the trip a very happy & enjoyable one, as well as beneficial to our health.

In the month of April 1877, I went to Charleston to spend a few weeks with my dear Parents, and while there my poor little Nina was taken with fever, a mild type of typhoid, it lasted nearly two weeks then, and hoping a change would break the fever, I

4. A popular beach resort in Chatham County, located 15 miles S.E. of Savannah on the south side of the entrance to the Savannah River.

brought her home, but it continued for nearly a month, & finally left her pale & thin in the extreme. The Dr. recommended a change of air, so we took her as far as St. Augustine, Florida. The sea trip strengthened her and on our return home she was quite bright again. She is my greatest care, dear little soul, she is so slight, so very delicate in appearance, and so very bright, that I have to be more careful of her than of my others, who are very strong and hearty. She is seldom a half hour from me, and is chatting & playing by my side, by the hour, in the afternoons, after her bath, she is dressed and plays on the green in front of the house.

Yesterday when I opened the door and told her to run and play with "Bessie" across the street, she looked out and said, "No, I see free of my feethearts playing in the dirt, I vasser go there." Sure enough there were seated in the sand, Masters - Gordin Guerard, Horace Crane & Eddie Munnerlyn—the three sweethearts of Miss Pauline Heyward.

Savannah, Ga., July, 1878

A year has gone by since my last records. A year unmarked by any momentous events to my little crew. Always a remarkably healthy & thriving family, it came somewhat hard upon us all, when the diseases incident to childhood made their appearance amongst my bairns.

First, in *January, '78,* the three girls had a pretty severe attack of *diptheric* sore throat. The boy (Jack we call him) escaped, as I kept him strictly apart. And after about two weeks' nursing, my little girls recovered, and we had a run of health until, MARCH, '78, when Elise & Jack were strickened with measles, they were both very sick, particularly my Lieschin, who suffered much and was really very ill. Just as they were recovering, Maude & Pauline took it, they were well peppered, but were not so sick as the first attacks. They were scarcely well over the measles, before that distressing ailment—*whooping cough* made its appearance. My poor little Nina had it, as violently as any mortal child ever did, for five weeks she was a martyr, and lost all her flesh & being accompanied by a slow fever, which never left her for sixteen days, she was indeed reduced very low.

During all this time, my poor "pet lamb" was the object of my tenderest & untiring care, day & night. Jack's spell was next in violence, his teething made it very hard on him, and being a young chap of great vehemence, he would lose all patience, & show fight in the most furious manner to the nearest person, as soon as a paroxysm would come on, thereby almost suffocating himself. My elder girls had it distressingly but by no means violently. Even now it lingers amongst them all & every day or so, someone will have an attack of coughing, from APRIL it has lasted until JULY.

Jack teethed with great trouble to himself, a spell of sickness with each tooth, but like Maude, he lost no flesh, and he is now as fine a specimen for a two-year-old as can be seen anywhere. Not a beauty, but a magnificently formed fellow, with handsome grey eyes, and a countenance—young as he is—worth untold riches for the clear, frank truth, it expresses, full of life & intelligence & affectionate & warm hearted as possible. All in all, I would not change my fair haired son in a single respect.

Savannah, Ga., May, 1880

As the little folks grow, the old ones have less time for amusements or ought else beyond the duties required of them by a growing family, consequently the little book of "Records," has been put by for many months, whereas the family history goes on replete with important events.

As I purpose registering each spell of sickness, I must mention a severe spell of fever, Malarial in nature, which reduced our Maude's immaculate pink & white flesh, to half its quantity, and the extreme heat of the summer (1879) determined her dear Father upon sending us all off to get some mountain air. As ever with him, he forgot his own loneliness & discomfort in being without his family, in his desire for their welfare and enjoyment. And before we had time to discuss all the pro's & con's, we found ourselves on the way up to the Warm Springs in N.C. reveling in the exquisite beauty of the scenery on the French Broad,[5] and the little ones getting fat & rosy in the delicious climate.

5. The Warm Springs of Buncombe County, located on the western bank of the French Broad River, was one of the most notable of the springs of North Carolina.

We were there two months, and as usual my children were considered the *handsomest set,* amongst the very many there.

Master Jack became a perfect little mountaineer, and did all but tumble himself into the rocky little river.

On our return home, hearty and refreshed, our girls started school with renewed vigor, little Nina, now 5 years old, began school at Miss Belle Heit's so that Jack & I were left alone to bear each other company all thro the winter days, he was my little escort whenever I went out, and we worked to-gether in the garden, for hours at a time, he calling himself, "Captain Waterman," taking especial delight in keeping the water pot filled for me.

All went happily until December, when my lady Maude must needs frighten the wits out of us by an attack of genuine diptheria, she was never *very ill,* but quite enough so to fill our hearts with great anxiety. We kept her entirely apart from the others, & while nursing her, I only took flying peeps at my other nestlings; thus we prevented their taking the dread disease, and after three weeks exile, Maude returned, quite restored, to her roost in the nursery.

Elise shortly after had a spell of ulcerated sore throat & fever, she was very sick for a week, then no more sickness, save the ordinary colds & toothaches for a long time. One sweet spring morning, the 22nd of March, 1880, the greatest possible excitement prevailed in the house of Heyward, when the little folks all came home from paying a visit to their Aunts, it was announced to them that a baby brother had arrived during their absence. They could not realize such good news until they saw with their own eyes, one of the loveliest spring babies ever seen, & heard that he had come to be their dear little brother FRANK.

Chapter Fifteen

Family Life:
Joys and Sorrows

October 1882

Two long sad years have passed over us, and I have not dared to register the event which has filled my heart to overflowing. We found that uncertainty of life's happiness, when after a fearful illness of a month's duration, we realized the fact that our life's pride & deep joy was only lent to us, that God had recalled the priceless gift of our first son, and Jack, my precious, my idol was taken from me. How can I write it, even now, that my boy is gone from me forever, the agony of this thought never leaves my heart, and seldom can I trust myself on this subject, so rebellious is this sinful heart, so great is its yearning for the child who has gone. Meningitis, they called it, God alone knows what it was that struck him down in the midst of his vigor & splendid health, or why it was that so noble & vigorous a child should so suffer & die! I must not touch on this subject, for then I lose control of myself. I must simply record our bitter bereavement & lock my heart again. It happened on the 12th of January, 1881. The saddest day I ever knew.

We have had no illness since our darling Jack's, and God has blessed us in the children who are spared—but Oh! what trembling joys they are to me now, how uncertain I feel when I call them *mine.*

Elise has grown into a beautiful, attractive girl, in her fifteenth year, with such a coterie of admirers & youthful aspirants for her smiles, that we saw plainly how her education & freshness would suffer, unless for a time removed from these interruptions, so we have placed her at school in the beautiful convent of Mount de Sales in Maryland.[1] She is perfectly happy there & in her

---

1. The name of this convent school was undoubtedly derived from the Society of St. Francis de Sales, popularly known as the Salesians, a religious group

usual happy manner has made many warm friends, she possesses to a rare extent that wonderful gift of attractiveness.

Maude is unusually well grown for her age, eleven, she is a handsome English looking girl, full of the finest traits of character & is the promise of a very noble woman.

Nina is carrying out all her baby promise of rare sweetness, talent & originality, she is very bright and every inch a *dainty little lady*.

And Frank, now our only boy, is a beautiful strong fellow, in his third year, filled with the spirit of mischief, high tempered, warm hearted and in many respects, exactly like Jack. Altho very handsome, not as splendidly formed & strong as Jack was at his age. He is a wonderful comfort to us, altho the void can never be filled.

[1883]

On 22d NOVEMBER, 1882, a lovely dainty little daughter came to us, we called her Ethel, because it is a lovely name and suited her; she was a perfect little pearl in beauty and sweetness, very bright & playful, altho delicate. She did not stay with us but went up to join our little band in Heaven; after a very short sickness of three days from dysentery, she left us on the night 9th of MAY, 1883 precious little Ethel. God lent her to us just long enough to make us wrap our hearts around her. Where these treasures go, there also must be our hearts. Nina was the little God-mother.

In the spring of 1883 Frank had measles & a long spell of fever. When baby Ethel left us, I would not have a nurse for Frank, but devoted myself to him, and there were very few moments that he was from my sight. A fine handsome boy, very impetuous, but a splendid heart.

September 9th, 1884

When "the Father" came home to dinner on this day, he found that during his absence a fine little chap had arrived. Mas-

devoted to the Christian education of youth. DeSales village was located in Baltimore County.

ter Walter Screven Heyward, with as much black hair on his head as he has name.

The little fellow was splendid & so heartily welcomed by his parents, his Grandmother & sisters & brother, that one might have thought he was the first baby. Well he is the first in the new house (Whitaker St.)[2] and most welcome is he. He grew right along, lost his crop of black hair, and substituted a growth of lovely brown and is called by every one a real "Beauty boy." Elise is his God-mother and she is wild over him.

This young lady having gone thro a three years' course at Mt. de Sales, returned to us in the early summer of 1885, a young lady. A sweet pure hearted child, fulfilling all her early promises of being lovely in mind and body. I am *so happy* in her, and look forward to her companionship, as one of my chief joys. So many years of my life have been spent (and still are filled by) the divided joys and sorrows and cares of the nursery, that I can scarcely realize that I have a grown child to bless me now. And Maude is a fourteen-year-old comfort and joy to me. Almost grown in size, and with a fine resolute character; the favorite of a large circle of friends.

Nina is stronger & heartier than she has ever been, very pretty and very precise, she attempts always to express herself with the largest words she can find, and is very circumstantial and full of anecdote, which gives us a great deal of amusement.

We live chiefly for our children and have no joys outside of the home. Guerard is the fondest & most indulgent Father I ever knew, and I do not think any children ever had a happier childhood than ours. Every now & then one of the girls is allowed to invite a friend & go over to Charleston and spend a week with Grandma & Grandpa, and this is always an event of such unmitigated enjoyment, that I am sure it will be to them one of the early joys that lurks in the remembrance all through life.

In AUGUST, 1885, Baby Walter had a severe illness, inflamation of the bowels, caused by cold & teething. We were very wretched & spent many sleepless nights working for his life. With the bitter experience we have had, we are utterly miserable &

---

2. Guerard Heyward had a new home built on Whitaker Street in 1883 for his growing family. This home is still extant, operating as an inn, and is located next to Hodgson Hall, which houses the Georgia Historical Society.

alarmed when an illness comes to one of them. God, in this instance, mercifully spared him to us to be a strength and comfort to me in my declining years.

Walter has 8 teeth, is now 11 months old.

In SEPTEMBER, 1884, Nina had an attack of malarial fever which lasted nearly three weeks & reduced her much.

Elise went with Auntie [Rose] in July, 1885 to the White Sulphur Springs, W. Va.,[3] her first jaunt as young lady, this I should so much have wished to share, but babies cannot go around with young ladies, so Walter & I remained at home.

Maude had a summer's trip to Griffin,[4] returned fresh & sweet as a rose, and Nina with her friend, May Godwin, visited Grandma.

We dear old folks? & boys remained at home.

October 1885

Frank had an illness of five weeks, a blood disease, called Purpera Hemorngheta [Hemorrhagica], not dangerous, but exceedingly painful and tedious. He bore it like a little man, indeed he is very brave in bearing pain, and while he is naturally of an impetuous and impatient nature, I am proud to see that young as he is, he shows great determination & fortitude when occasion requires. Frank possesses a fine heart & nature and with these and the most earnest heart prayers of his Mother, he must surely turn out the noble man I picture him in the future. I kneel by his little bed at night and look upon his beautiful innocent face, and I freely offer *my* life to God to gain from Him the strength & moral courage for my precious boy, that will enable him to pass thro life's temptations into a pure & fine manhood.

---

3. White Sulphur Springs in Greenbrier County, W. Va., one of the largest and most fashionable spas, was noted for the curative powers of its mineral waters.
4. Griffin, the capital of Spalding County, Georgia, 43 miles south of Atlanta on the Central of Georgia and Southern Railroad lines, was noted as a marketing center for cotton.

The Summer of 1886

I spent at the Old Sweet Springs in W. Va.,[5] the mountain air braced them all up, & while in that section I took them to visit the beautiful caverns of Luray [Virginia], this interested them all, especially Maude, who delights in the investigation of mysteries.

Walter was considered the handsomest child at the Springs, and indeed my heart throbs with *pride*, when I look at my pretty boys. I brought them home to their dear Father pictures of good health & happiness.

In NOVEMBER, 1886, Frank had an attack of errysipilis and was quite ill for a week or two, when he recovered he started school with Miss Grady & soon learned to read.

September 1887

Just now our happly little band is separating for a time, and this brings sadness to my heart. As long as we are to-gether, everything goes well, but these partings try me dreadfully.

First, Maude is to go on to a finishing school in N.Y. I have promised her from the first to go on with her, the child loves me very much, and I feel that I am a strength & a comfort to her, & she is certainly the same to me, so I will go with her, but then I must leave my others. Nina we have sent to Northern Ga. where the climate is splendid, & where we hope she will wax strong & well; she is very happy there. And this morning I went to the depot & put my two little precious pets, my baby boys, on the cars with their nurse, Affy, to go to Charleston to their loving & beloved Grandparents, they will remain there in their kind hands until my return from N.Y., where I am to leave my Maude. Elise will go with us, she is such an experienced little traveler, that she will be invaluable to us, especially as is generally the case, in our trips, their dear Father cannot go with us.

We are to sail on 7th. I wish it were all over & I back at home. My heart is very full at parting with my babies, the house seems unnatural & too still, and old goose that I am, I had many a cry

5. The Sweet Springs, discovered in 1764, is located in Monroe County, West Virginia, 17 miles southeast of White Sulphur Springs.

over it to-day, then comes the parting with Maude, and my Nina is sadly missed, I am not made for all these things. God made me for a home Mother where my joy is to have my darlings with me, & to be *there always* for them; there *in* the home are all my joys, my life, my love, in with my very heart, where its fondest hopes and most fervent prayers are concentrated.

Finis. March 5th, 1888

[Death of Pauline's beloved husband, Jacob Guerard Heyward][6]

6. Jacob Guerard Heyward died suddenly, March 5, 1888, at home after ingesting a large amount of seafood which apparently caused an anaphylactic reaction cutting off his air supply. His attending physician, Dr. Read, listed cause of death as "Oedema of Glottis." He had a known history of allergy to shellfish.

Epilogue

Guerard Heyward's sudden death at age forty-four was a shattering blow to his large family. He had been, without question, the keystone of the Heyward clan following his father's death. In 1868 he had obtained a job in Savannah as a bookkeeper with Bates & Comer. Soon after establishing himself there he had moved his family into a home nearby, helped the older boys find gainful employment, and assisted the younger children in getting an education. Guerard was an astute businessman and by 1877 was a partner in the firm of H. M. Comer & Co., cotton and rice factors.

According to Pauline's father, Guerard's "too generous purse was ever open to all who needed help, even as we have since found to be very large amounts, and where he knew a return could never be made."[1] Guerard's death reduced his family from a life of ease to one of comparative poverty. Although Pauline's reaction to Guerard's death was that her life was over, she also realized the immediate necessity of generating income to support her five children. Within a week after Guerard's death, Pauline had converted her large home into a boarding house.

In June of 1888 Pauline wrote to her Aunt Rose: "It was the sweetest & most cherished delusion of my life to think that my Guerard & I would be here, strong & able to be the rest & prop for you, dearly loved ones when need be! & now how utterly turned are the tables: Now my strength has turned to weakness: My joy to bitterness: but I will struggle on to the very end for the dear ones, my little ones and my old ones; and sometimes I feel that God will help me: Then again, I am so appalled by all that has befallen me that despair gets the better of me! I don't dare think! or I find that all my strength is superficial, and I am nothing after all but a poor broken hearted creature! But enough of this: I am throwing myself off my balance terribly and there is yet much to do!"[2] Pauline underestimated her own strength. The pluck and spirit she had evinced as a young woman during the war had

---

1. DeCaradeuc Papers 1497, SHC: Memoir of Achille DeCaradeuc.
2. *Ibid.* Copy of a letter from Pauline to her Aunt Rose della Torre.

become sublimated over the years as she fulfilled the role of wife and mother within the confines of the society of her day. Faced with the crisis of economic survival, Pauline once again drew upon her inner strength. Her children relied on her. With hard work, the receipt of a modest life insurance payment, and the help of her older daughters, Pauline managed to support her family.

Her life went on. On December 31, 1890, Elise married Dr. John Smallbrook Howkins, M.D. The wedding ceremony took place at the DeCaradeuc home with the Catholic Bishop Thomas A. Becker officiating. The young couple lived with Pauline until 1900, when they moved into a new office/home. On August 23, 1892, Elise presented Pauline with her first grandchild, John S. Howkins, Jr. Elise later had another son, Guerard Heyward Howkins. On April 25, 1894, Nina married Arthur Overton in a wedding at the Cathedral of St. John the Baptist, Savannah, with Fr. J. S. McCarthy officiating. It was Nina who, although in delicate health, presented Pauline with a granddaughter who was named Pauline after her grandmother.

In 1895 her beloved father, Achille DeCaradeuc, died in Charleston. Her mother, Elizabeth Ann DeCaradeuc, paid frequent visits to Pauline, but continued to live in her home in Charleston with her nephew, Thomas della Torre, and grandson, St. Julien DeCaradeuc Jr., until her death in 1905.[3] Pauline faced yet another tragedy when in 1909 her daughter Nina, whose delicate constitution had been a continued source of concern for her mother, died at age thirty-five of Bright's disease.

Pauline continued to provide a home for her family throughout the years, even after she moved in 1906 into another residence, this one on Gwinnett Street. Her daughter Maude remained single, pursued a career as a librarian, and lived with her mother, lending support and comfort. Arthur Overton stayed in Pauline's home with his little daughter after Nina's death. Frank had married and moved into his own home, but Walter continued living at home until 1912. And the following year, Elise, recently widowed, returned home with her two young sons.

Pauline DeCaradeuc Heyward, surrounded by her loving family, died at the age of sixty-nine on January 28, 1914, of chronic endocarditis and acute bronchitis. Her death notice read simply: "Heyward—died Jan. 28, 1914, fortified by the sacraments of the

3. DeCaradeuc Papers 1497, SHC: Tribute. . . .

church, Pauline DeCaradeuc Heyward, widow of J. Guerard Hey-
ward." Her funeral was held at the Cathedral of St. John the
Baptist, and she was buried next to Guerard in Laurel Grove
Cemetery, in Savannah.[4]

Her life stands as a striking affirmation of the female role as
envisioned by nineteenth-century American society. There was
never a more devoted wife and mother. But the strength, courage,
and resourcefulness of this "Confederate Lady" as she faced the
hardships and tragedies of her life certainly belie the limited role
into which her gender had cast her.

4. Chatham County, Georgia Department of Vital Records, Death Record of Pauline D. Heyward, 28 January 1914; *Savannah Morning News*, Jan. 29 and Jan.
30, 1914.

Bibliography

Manuscripts

Alderman Library, University of Virginia, Special Collection: Speech of General Henry A. Wise, 1874

Archives, Diocese of Savannah: RG 2, Series 1, History of the Diocese; RG 2, Series 1.1, Registers

Chatham County, Georgia, Department of Vital Records: Death Records

Edgefield, South Carolina, Courtesy Center and Archives: Agatha A. Woodson, Confederate Scrapbook

Georgia Historical Society, Savannah
DeCaradeuc Family Papers
Georgia Collection: Georgia Pamphlets, Vol. 6
Heyward–Howkins Family Papers
Joseph Clay Habersham Paper

South Carolina Department of Archives and History: South Carolina Census Records

South Carolina Historical Society, Charleston
DeCaradeuc Family Papers
Thomas della Torre Papers
Isaac Hayne Journal 1764–1822
Heyward Family Papers
William Henry Johnson, St. Thomas and St. Denis Parishes Scrapbook
Map of Charleston District, 1820
Map Showing Plantations along the Cooper River, 1842
Robert Mills Atlas of the State of South Carolina, 1781–1855
St. Thomas Parish, Charleston District, Plat 1812
St. Thomas Parish, Charleston District, Plat 1906

Southern Historical Collection, Wilson Library, University of North Carolina
John Hamilton Cornish Papers
DeCaradeuc Papers

147

City Directories

Charleston

The Charleston Directory and Register for 1835–6.
The Charleston Directory and Strangers' Guide for 1840.
A Directory of the City of Charleston and Neck for 1849.
Directory for the City of Charleston for the Year 1852.
Charleston City Directory 1875–6.
Sholes' Directory of the City of Charleston for 1877–78; 1882; 1884; 1887.

Savannah

Purse's Directory of the City of Savannah, 1866.
Savannah City Directory for 1867.
Abrams' Directory of the City of Savannah for 1870.
Haddock's Savannah, Ga. Directory, 1871.
Estill's Savannah Directory, 1874–5.
Abrams' Savannah Directory, 1876–7.
Rogers City Directory of Savannah, 1877.
Sholes' Directory of the City of Savannah, Vol. I, 1879.
————. *Savannah Directory, Vol. II, 1880.*
————. *Directory of the City of Savannah, 1881.*
————. *Savannah Directory, Vol. VI, 1884.*
————. *Directory of the City of Savannah, Vol. IX, 1888.*
————. *Directory of the City of Savannah, Vol. X, 1889.*
————. *Directory of the City of Savannah, Vol. XIX, 1898.*
————. *Directory of the City of Savannah, Vol. XX, 1899.*
————. *Directory of the City of Savannah, Vol. XXI, 1900.*
Goette's Savannah City Directory for 1904; 1906; 1907.
Savannah City Directory, 1911; 1913.

Other Primary Sources

Annals of Savannah, 1850–1937, A Digest of the Newspaper Record of Events and Opinions, Vol 26, Abstracts From the Files of the *Savannah Morning News* of 1875, Savannah, 1968.

Bleser, Carol, ed. *Secret and Sacred: The Diaries of James Henry Hammond, A Southern Slaveholder.* New York: Oxford University Press, 1988.

Brooks, U. R. *South Carolina Bench and Bar.* Columbia: The State Co., 1908.

Caldwell, J. F. J. *The History of a Brigade of South Carolinians Known First as Gregg's Brigade and Subsequently as McGowan's Brigade.* Philadelphia: King & Baird Printers, 1866; rpt., Marietta, GA: The Continental Book Co., 1951.

Clute, Robert F., "The Annals and Parish Register of St. Thomas and St. Denis Parish in South Carolina From 1860 to 1884," (Charleston: Walker, Evans & Cogswell Printers, 1884), SCHS File 20–40.

Cyclopedia of Eminent and Representative Men of the Carolinas in the Nineteenth Century. Madison: Brant and Fuller, 1892.

Deming Henry C. *The Life of Ulysses S. Grant, U. S. Army.* Hartford: S. S Scranton & Co., 1868.

Evans, Clement, ed. *Confederate Military History.* Atlanta: 1899; rpt., New York: Thomas Yoseloff, 1962. Abbreviated as *CMH.*

Filby, P. William, with Mary K. Meyer, eds. *Passenger and Immigration Lists Index*, 1st ed,. 1982 Supplement. Detroit: Gale Research Co., 1983.

Gallagher, Gary W., ed. *Fighting for the Confederacy: The Personal Recollections of General Edward Porter Alexander.* Chapel Hill: University of North Carolina Press, 1989.

Garlington, J. C. *Men of the Time: Sketches of Living Notables, A Biographical Encyclopedia of Contemporaneous South Carolina Leaders.* Spartanburg: Garlington Publishing Co., 1902.

"The Heyward Family Burying Ground at Old House Near Grahamville, S. C." *The South Carolina Historical and Genealogical Magazine,* 41 (April 1940): 75–80.

"Heyward Genealogy." *The South Carolina Historical and Genealogical Magazine,* 59 (1958): 206, 211.

Heyward, James Barnwell, II. *Heyward Family.* Privately Published, 1925.

Holcomb, Brent H., comp. *Marriages and Death Notices from the Charleston Times.* Baltimore: Genealogical Publishing Co., 1979.

——, G.R.S., *Probate Records of South Carolina,* Vol. 2. Easley, SC: Southern Historical Press, 1978.

Jervey, Elizabeth Heyward. "From Marriage and Death Notices from the City Gazette of Charleston, South Carolina." *The South Carolina Historical Magazine,* 48 (1947): 77.

Jones, Charles C., Jr. *History of Savannah, Georgia.* Syracuse: 1890.

Long, A. L. *Memoirs of Robert E. Lee, His Military and Personal History.* New York: J. M. Stoddart, 1887.

Moorman, J. J. *The Virginia Springs and Springs of the South and West.* Philadelphia: Lippincott & Co., 1859.

Obituary Addresses Delivered on the Death of the Honorable Franklin H. Elmore in the Senate and House of Representatives of the United States, May 30 and 31, 1850. The South Caroliniana Library, University of South Carolina.

O'Connell, J. J. *Catholicity in the Carolinas and Georgia: Leaves of Its History.* New York: D & J. Sadlier, 1879.

O'Neall, John Belton. *Bench and Bar of South Carolina, Vol. II,* 1859. Spartanburg: The Reprint Co., 1975.

OR. See *War of the Rebellion.*

Parton, James. *General Butler in New Orleans: History of the Administration of the Department of the Gulf in the Year 1862.* New York: Mason Bros., 1864.

Salley, A. S., Jr., comp. *South Carolina Troops in Confederate Service.* Columbia: The State Co., 1914.

Schirmer, Jacob Frederick. "From the Schirmer Diary." *The South Carolina Historical Magazine,* 70, 1 (1969): 62.

Sherwood, Adiel. *A Gazetteer of the State of Georgia,* 3rd ed. Washington City: P. Force, 1877.

Sholes, A. E., comp. *Chronological History of Savannah from Its Settlement by Oglethorpe down to December 31, 1899, Together with a Complete Record of the City and County and Savannah's Roll of Honor, a Roster of the Soldiers Who Have in Three Wars Gone Forth at Their Country's Call from This City.* Savannah: The Morning News Print, 1900; rpt., Savannah: Kennickell Printing Co., 1975.

Von Borcke, Heros. *Memoirs of the Confederate War for Independence.* New York: Lippincott, 1866; rpt. Peter Smith, 1938.

War of the Rebellion: A Compilation of the Official Records of the Union and Confederate Armies. Washington: Government Printing Office, 1880–1901. Abbreviated as *OR.*

War of the Rebellion: The Official Records of the Union and Confederate Navies. Washington: Government Printing Office, 1897. Abbreviated as *ORN.*

Webber, Mabel L. "Copy of Some Loose Pages Found among the Manigault Papers in the Handwriting of Dr. Gabriel Manigault, October 25, 1888." *The South Carolina Historical and Genealogical Magazine,* 40 (1939): 16.

Works Progress Administration. *Cemetery Inscriptions, Aiken County, South Carolina.* Columbia: 1949.

Works Progress Administration, *Laurel Grove Cemetery, Savannah, Georgia, 1852–1938.* Vol. II, G–M, Savannah, 1939.

United States Census Reports

1800
District of Charleston, South Carolina.
1850
The Parishes of St. Philip's and St. Michael's in the District of Charleston, South Carolina.
St. Helena Parish, Town of Beaufort, Beaufort County, South Carolina.
Columbia, Richland County, South Carolina.
Barnwell County, South Carolina.
1860
Free Schedules, Aiken, Barnwell District, South Carolina.
Slave Schedules, Abbeville, Anderson and Barnwell Districts, South Carolina.
4th Ward, City of Augusta, Richmond County, Georgia.
Columbia County, Georgia.
Columbia, Richland County, South Carolina.
Columbia Female College, Richland County, South Carolina.
Graniteville, Edgefield District, South Carolina.
Laurensville, Laurens Court House, South Carolina.
City of Savannah, Chatham County, Georgia.
1870
St. Peter's Parish, Post Office, Bluffton, Beaufort County, South Carolina.
Columbia, Richland County, South Carolina.

Newspapers

The Charleston Daily Courier.
The Charleston Mercury.
The Daily News and Herald (Savannah).
The Edgefield (South Carolina) Advertiser.
The Morning News (Savannah).
The Richmond Enquirer.

Secondary Sources

Barnhart, Clarence L., ed. *The New Century Cyclopedia of Names.* Englewood Cliffs, NJ: Prentice-Hall, 1954.

Caldwell, Benjamin Palmer, Jr., ed. *No. II, A Longer Short History of Bluffton, South Carolina and Its Environs.* Hilton Head: Impressions Printing Co., 1988.

Derrick, Samuel Melanchthon. *Centennial History of the South Carolina Railroad.* Columbia: The State Co., 1930; rpt., Spartanburg: The Reprint Co., 1975.

Faust, Patricia L., ed. *Historical Times Illustrated Encyclopedia of the Civil War.* New York: Harper & Row, 1986.

"George W. Croft of the Citadel Cadets." *Confederate Veteran* 23 (1915): 366.

Gannett, Henry, *A Gazetteer of Maryland and Baltimore.* Baltimore: Genealogical Publishing Co., 1976.

Graydon, Nell S. *Tales of Beaufort.* Beaufort: Beaufort Book Shop, 1963.

Hattaway, Herman, and Archer Jones. *How the North Won: A Military History of the Civil War.* Urbana: University of Illinois Press, 1983.

Heilprin, Angelo, and Louis Heilprin, eds. *Lippincott's New Gazetteer: A Complete Pronouncing Gazetteer or Geographical Dictionary of the World.* Philadelphia: Lippincott, 1931.

Hennig, Helen Kohn, ed. *Columbia, Capital City of South Carolina.* Columbia: Sesqui-Centennial Commission, 1936.

History of Saint Mary Help of Christians Church and the Aiken Missions. Compiled for the Seventy-fifth Anniversary Diamond Jubilee. Aiken County Public Library, 1942.

Hubbell, Jay B. *The South in American Literature, 1607–1900.* Durham: Duke University Press, 1954.

Irving, John B. *A Day on the Cooper River*. 3rd ed. Enlarged and edited by Louisa Cheves Stoney. Columbia: Press of the R. L. Bryan Co., 1969.

Kovacik, Charles F., and John J. Winberry. *South Carolina, A Geography*. Boulder/London: Westview Press, 1987.

Morrison, Mary L., ed. *Historic Savannah: Survey of Significant Buildings in the Historic and Victorian Districts of Savannah, Georgia*. 2nd ed. Savannah: Historic Savannah Foundation and the Junior League of Savannah, 1979.

Neuffer, Claude Henry, ed. *Names in South Carolina*, Vols. 1–18. Columbia: The State Printing Co., 1954–78.

Seig, Chan. *The Squares: An Introduction to Savannah*. Norfolk/Virginia Beach: The Donning Co., 1984.

South Carolina Genealogies, Articles from the South Carolina History (and Genealogy) Magazine. Spartanburg: The Reprint Co., published in association with the South Carolina Historical Society, 1983.

Williams, T. Harry. *P. G. T. Beauregard, Napoleon in Gray* (Baton Rouge: Louisiana State University Press, 1955.

Wise, Stephen R. *Lifeline of the Confederacy: Blockade Running during the Civil War*. Columbia: University of South Carolina Press, 1988.

Index

Ga. Artillery Battery (Nelson's Brigade), 51n
Jeff Davis Legion, 77n
Maxwell's Battery, Ga. Artillery, 43n
Palmetto Sharpshooters (Jenkins' Brigade), 48n
7th S.C. Battalion, 47n
3rd S.C. Cavalry, 9n
3rd S.C. Volunteers, 47n
34th Va. Volunteers, 37n, 47
28th Georgia, 24n;
25th S.C. Volunteers, 16n, 46n
Wise's Infantry Brigade, 46 and n, 50
Milledge, Joe, 94
Milledge, Capt. John, Jr., 8, 51 and n, 55–56, 77, 83, 94
Milroy, Gen. Robert, 18n
Molineux, Gen. Edward L., 7, 80 and n, 81
Montmorenci, 1, 6 and n, 7, 10–11, 119, 123–24
Morrell, Fannie, 41
Morrell, John, 24 and n
Morris Island, S.C., 21 and n, 22, 23 and n, 24 and n, 25n, 26, 84n
Mount de Sales, Convent of, 136 and n, 138

New Orleans, La., 34 and n, 75n
New River, 115
New York, 103, 124, 140
Ney, Edgar, 4
Ney, Marshall Michel, 4

O'Driscoll, Frank, 144
O'Driscoll, Mr. and Mrs. W. C., 42 and n
Old Sweet Springs, W. Va., 139 and n
Overton, Arthur, 144
Overton, Pauline, 144

Parrott, Fannie, xxi, 78n, 84
Parrott, Flint, xxi, 78n, 79
Parrott, Julia, xxi, 77, 83, 78n
Parrott, William, xxi, 78n
Parrott Family, 78, 105
Pemberton, Gen. John C., 15 and n, 21 and n
Persico, Bishop Ignatio, 8n
Petersburg, Va., 50–51
Piedmont Hotel (Gainesville, Ga.), 130
Pleasonton, Gen. Alfred, 18n

Port Hudson, La., 19n
Prendergast, J. J., 42n
Prendergast, Mrs. 42, 43
Price, Gen. Sterling, 21 and n
Pulaski House (Savannah, Ga.), 119

Rappahannock River, 18 and n
Redmond, Mel, xxi, 55, 93–94, 103, 105
Redmond, Nellie, xxi, 52, 55–56, 81, 93, 96
Redmond Family, 51 and n, 103
Rhett, Col. Alfred, 25 and n
Rhett, Robert Barnwell, Jr., 85 and n
Rhett, Robert Barnwell, Sr., 85n
Richardson, Lt. W. S., 44 and n
Richmond, Va., 50, 57
Ripley, Gen. R.S., 25n
Rocheblanche, Louise Agathe de la Toison, xviii, 3
Rose Hill, 24 and n, 41, 59
Ruxton, Augustus, 119

St. Augustine, Fla., 133
St. Thomas Parish (Charleston District), 3
Sandhills Village, Ga., 51 and n
San Jacinto. See Trent Affair
Santo Domingo, 2, 5
Savannah, Ga., 7, 27, 41–43, 45, 76, 119–20, 127, 129–30, 145; Sherman occupies, 61
Schwartz, Dr. and Mrs. U. B., 84 and n
Servants: Old Peter, 114; Affy (nurse), 140;
Seward, William Henry, 74 and n
Sherman, Gen. William T., 69, 74n; occupies Columbia, 70 and n; occupies Savannah, 61 and n
Shooter, Lt. Col. Washington P., 46 and n
Siegfried & Co., 120
Simmons, Fannie, 88
Slaves: Jabe, xxi, 51; Joe, xxi, 75, 80–81; Solomon, xxi, 67; William, xxi, 69; freed in Augusta, 77; from Santo Domingo, 3, 10, 101n; loyalty of, 67–68, 80; at Montmorenci, 6
Slidell, John. See Trent Affair
Smith, Gen. Kirby, 75n
Soldiers: black troops: in New Orleans, 34; in Aiken, 79; guard Montmorenci, 80–82 and n; Federal: deserters, 61; Kilpatrick's troops